## About the Author

Johnny Bluhazy was born in 1992, in England. Due to a turbulent childhood, he has lived in many counties south of the country and has spent much time travelling in foreign lands as well. Living somewhat of an unconventional life, experiencing many different things, Johnny has found his passion in creative writing and wishes to go on expressing himself in this way.

# Home

# Johnny Bluhazy

# Home

Olympia Publishers
*London*

**www.olympiapublishers.com**
OLYMPIA PAPERBACK EDITION

A CIP catalogue record for this title is
available from the British Library.

ISBN: 978-1-78830-748-2

This is a work of fiction.
Names, characters, places and incidents originate from the writer's
imagination. Any resemblance to actual persons, living or dead, is
purely coincidental.

First Published in 2021

Olympia Publishers
Tallis House
2 Tallis Street
London
EC4Y 0AB
Printed in Great Britain

# Dedication

In loving memory of my mother, Tina

# Acknowledgements

There is not one person I know who I would not give thanks to, in some way or another.

# Chapter One

**Blue.**

I live for the rawness in the heart of man.

The screams for his freedom etch on the edge of his sanity
And there will come a time when he breaks, truthfully,
Into the senses of those who have continued to fear
And forgotten how to love.

**Black.**

It may never make sense but with this you have to try. Get it down and get it out? I am afraid to.

Express yourself! Why would you be afraid to?

What if all I say and all I do is nothing more than a lie? Sometimes, and you know this, I am to feel like it is.

**Red.**

An inevitable living death is written on the hands of those whom have been misunderstood and forsaken in their gift by those whom walk around him in slumber. 'Jesus Christ,' I shout out aloud in anger. As a child, sleep was the last thing I had wanted. I had wanted to live. Be out there. Not within this darkness which we eternally fear right here in our existence.

Why then, as the years pass onto my age, have I resorted back to a torpor through the days and nights by which I breathe silently and unwillingly?

It is like a parallel to the misted sky of night, posing an impossibility to see the constellations above and like the truth of a shadow to a ghost. Purpose fluctuates in the strangest of ways and I only know one purpose here. My eyes which were once wide open are now drawing closed and I do not want them to, I want to be able to see... I want to be able to see what is out there!

It is such that theatre has its light but the light must fade and the day has its sun but the sun must fall but tell me, is it true that we all must follow?

## Dead.

Twenty-five years have passed since I have walked through the gates of heaven into the beauty of life. Twenty-five years have passed and I have fallen into the jagged teeth of the prevailing beast. Outside I see the harsh howling blows of nature breathing heavily through the thick layers of darkness which lie dejected and depressed upon this cold and cruel earth.

Inside, it is now I feel myself imprisoned and contained to fear. Who am I to suffer in this dangerous and heedless pain? I sit alone in a room bare all but for four rats which scavenge around their cage for a little food and a little comfort. Suddenly, I am to witness my own reflection in the windowpane, longing lost into the torn sky of night. How woeful, I thought, it is to think.

## Truth.

What is it that you think?

Every man who has hated, has also loved.

## Tears.

'Get out,' he said. 'Go, just leave me.'

Tears begin to roll slowly down the side of her face as both children stand frightened, scared by her side. She very hesitantly looks over towards him.

'It wasn't supposed to be this way.'

'But you did, I know you did,' he shouts back angrily.

She looks away, guilty. The boy squeezes tight his mother's hand.

'I did everything for you,' he speaks again.

She lifts up her hand to try and dry away the tears from her eyes.

'No, you didn't,' her voice weak. 'You did it for yourself.'

The father suddenly picks up a family ornament and throws it at the wall ferociously. Fragile, it shatters into many pieces like a resemblance, like a sentiment to their marriage, to the vows they had once made to each other.

'Stop it.'

He storms over towards her. He grabs both children by their waists and lifts them up hastily into his arms in order to throw them onto each shoulder.

'Put them down!' the mother screams desperately.

He stares bitterly at her, 'You're on your own now, woman.'

He turns around to walk out of the door behind.

'Put them down,' she reaches out but he pushes her back.

In a moment all too sudden, the boy's head gets knocked against the wooden frame of the door and he falls heavily down to the ground.

'Look what you've done,' she cries.

'What I've done?' he then screams.

**Dust.**

I can remember when I was a child sitting on the floor in

the middle of the hall with all the others around me, every weekday morning. The teachers would talk and we would listen but I never listened and often got into trouble. Sometimes, I was made to stand and sometimes I was made to stay, but all the time I thought it to be unfair. I wasn't trying not to listen, I wasn't trying to be bad. I was just distracted. The curtains were only ever half drawn and the sun was always so bright; there the sun came through the tall windows to catch the dust in the light. And I can remember all the little particles dancing together and then alone, each to the same rhythm. In and out, back and forth, side to side, up and down. I was fascinated. I had thought to myself I could be one of the little particles as I watched the dust dance in the spaces above me and accidently ignored everything else.

**Light.**
>Nomadic mind
>Cloudless sky
>Hippie bird
>Flying high
>Circle chasing
>Rainbow rain
>Freedom come
>Gone again

**Life.**

Coming into life is something I do not keep possession of in my memory. I do ask myself if it would be necessary to know such an experience and I know not. However, I do know, and keep memory of, life coming into me.

**God.**

Have you ever considered what it is like to be alone with nothing but the few partial remains of your dimly lit heart and sorrowful soul? Have you ever considered the pitiful realisation that what you once had is no longer yours nor was it yours to begin with? Have you ever considered the possibility that your life is nothing but another apoplectic number against the will and nature of God? Have you ever considered the thought that nothing is real? Have you ever considered the mad idea that everything is?

**Mother.**

We lie together under the blue skies and make up things in the clouds which pass us by. Our minds run free and we laugh so loudly but most of the time we don't know why. I love her smile, it makes me smile and we share the same love for most of the things we know. She is my mother and I am her son and she told me she would never — never would she let me go.

**Father.**

I didn't know where we were going. I was just sitting on the back of this brand-new motorbike holding on for dear life, to my dad. It felt good. The bike looked good. It was bright red like the ones on television which race around the track really fast. We were going fast and it was fun. Really fun. We were riding down these old country lanes straight into rays of the sun and it seemed, only for a second, as if the world went on by without us.

**Trust.**

I trusted them with everything I had.

**Pain.**

God, who am I to try and explain this feeling I have? I don't understand it. I can't comprehend it. I just feel it. I feel it in the depths of my crying heart and wounded brain. If I am to tell you one thing, I will mean another and most often it will not be said at all. These dear, poor and helpless things I say will never be able to express this feeling I have for you. Why can't I express this feeling I have for you? When I eventually persuade the pen to touch paper and ask the ink to guide its way, soon enough I get pushed back into the darkness where blankness makes its stay. I could write until words no longer have meaning and letters are torn apart in war, this feeling will solemnly remain front row at my funeral, mourning to escape out from me and so desperate to find you, once more. Please God, help me!

**Scream.**

'Why am I here? Why? Tell me.' I scream out to you in desperation and you hear nothing of me. And after you have reduced me to nothing. You're not who they say you are. Only foolish am I to believe in something which has hidden from me like a spectre of the night. You have done nothing but emboss the voices in my head and wither my soul. 'Go from me,' I scream out into the vast empty spaces which cloud over my existence, 'Is this fair?'

**Out.**

The air is cold but the sun is warm
The fields are frosted but the light is bright
The trees have lost their leaves but they are still beautiful

16

nonetheless

Freedom lies within these country fields but not for the children ahead

## Help.

Their parents have engaged in yet another argument this evening. Shouting and screaming. It has now almost become something normal, something for the children to expect when they return home from school. It seems to be the parents have changed since their earlier days of knowing each other. The atmosphere around is so tense, all of the time. Home is no longer a home and there is no place here to take off their shoes and to still feel safe.

## Us.

The boy hides behind the cushions scared, hoping not to be seen. He isn't.

His sister hides quietly in her room upstairs, hoping to be ignored. She is.

## Please.

'Where did you go?' he said to her.

'For a walk with the children,' she said back to him.

'I saw you on the phone.'

My sister looked scared, nervous even. She understood more than I could.

'Yes, I had to make a phone call.'

'Who did you have to call?'

'A friend,' she said quietly.

'You're lying to me. Who did you call?'

'I've told you.'

'Tell me the truth.' He slammed down his fist on the table. Our mother paused into silence.

'I cannot believe you could do that to me,' he said.

'Please don't, not here,' she tried to say calmingly.

My sister had managed to leave the room and without asking. She would always try and hide whenever she thought that she might be in trouble.

'Please!' our mother reiterated to our father.

His face was full of anger and I was scared when he stood. I didn't know what was going to happen next; I didn't even know what was happening. 'I'm sorry, I am so sorry,' mother said.

I looked towards her, she was crying helplessly. Mother had called somebody on the phone earlier that day but I had not an idea who.

Father had walked away.

## Heed.

He always wanted the best
And the best is what he had
A wife, a house, a business
And the children: to be a dad.

## Hide.

They say silence is the worst. Silence is a time given to second-guess the next heart-breaking moment or to anxiously await the next sickening feeling inside the stomach. It can even be both at the same time sometimes.

That is why they hide, the children. They do not want to see the change in the faces which once was love but now fear and now hatred. They are to hope if they can close their eyes and pretend, the pain might just go away.

**Worry.**

If I am no longer dreaming, I am no longer here.

**Scared.**

How wonderful the life which is expressed in the ebb and flow of the sea and the sand, such a delightful place to be… with your family in hand…

There was a day when gentle waves soothed the body over and the bountiful sound of laughter lightened the heart of the soul. It was there, ahead of me, where the sun shone upon my mother and sister as they splashed around together in the water and I was to look on, to watch the things I loved most. I could see their happiness reflected in each other, like the sea dances glistens, and I could see an ease of life in the breeze which caught their hair as I was to sit lonely before them on the shore and smile.

But like the tears which mark an old photograph, we arrived home later that day to find blue lights flashing in the windows of our house and an ambulance parked outside the front of the driveway. Our home was to become a show highlighted in tragedy. It echoed an emptiness so dark and so heavy it felt like somebody had scribbled angrily in black crayon over my life just like a mistake is to be thrown away into the trash. The lights flashed bright into my eyes as our mother was to suddenly stop the car.

She ran inside, her face looking so afraid all I could do was fear the worst in her reaction. Everything turned to silence. My sister and I waited outside. Minutes passed by and nothing. Only a few moments later our father was to be hurried out of the house and placed into the back of the ambulance. To me, he looked dead. I cannot remember much of what happened after the ambulance had left and we were left, other than staring helplessly at the front of the house and at the door: number four.

What happened? I did not know at the time but I was to learn and, like

all children do, remember the feeling, the uncontrollable thinking, and...

I can remember a pain that had become inflamed within my heart. I had not one idea in which way I could turn or in which way I could just run.


**Sorry.**

Who could I blame for what was going to happen? My mother?

My father?

No, it was me. I had taken the blame. I had taken the blame. How can you blame somebody that you love?

I couldn't. I didn't. I was eight. It was when I first learnt hate.

Hate not of them, hate of me and little did I know it was to stick with me. With me until now.

How? Hate?

Well, I was given a choice. A choice?

They said to me, 'Son, you have a decision to make.'

Now I remember, it wasn't even them.

Then who?

It was a man, he was strange to me.

He looked me in the eyes and said, 'Please listen. Your mother and father are getting a divorce and we need to know who you are going to live with.'

At that moment, I burst out crying.

To decide, I didn't even want to start trying.

But I did. I chose Mum. And my sister chose her too.

I guess that was a very hard thing to do.

And I thought about my dad: how was he supposed to feel?

What was he supposed to think?

So, you had taken the blame and let the guilt inside sink? How can you blame somebody that you love?

It is a very good question.

So much has happened since then, I don't even know where to start. Well, I think you know that you've got a good brain and a good heart.

# Chapter Two

**Don't be sorry.**

The boy was called in for disciplinary. He had recently been acting in ways different to the others and it was certainly proving evident in his behaviour and temperament. Stress was causing anger. Rage was causing violence. He was to be known before as one of the quiet ones, but now the boy, in no surprising way, was to become an outward expression of the emotion he can no longer contain in the quiet corners of the classroom.

His once easy and kind nature has now been substituted for offense and disorder as the school playground provides opportunity to create plays of chaos and chances to inflict his pain upon the others. To graffiti the walls and faces of the public has now become the best way in which he can express himself, unseen yet noticed while to take and steal from people is his way of getting back what he feels he has lost or worse, stolen from him.

**Really?**

Please try not to be too real for you will lose half of what is.

**No.**

It had only been a matter of days between making the

decision and then being taken into a new home, or what was supposed to be a new home. My mother had taken my sister and I to live someplace away from our father, which actually happened to be just around the corner, in order to start a new beginning and a new way of life she thought better. However, it was still very important to her that my sister and I kept a close relationship with him even though she concluded it was time for her to try to move on.

That is a fair thing to do. I suppose.

I cannot remember the day I had to leave him though. My next memory was sitting around the dining room table for dinner at our new house, us three and this other man. The man, who sat opposite me, was tall, built. He had long hair, his demeanour stern and his voice deep. I was not to know who he was before and I had not one idea that he was going to be there with us, but I can remember feeling really uncomfortable around him. I had thought to myself it was most probably best to just keep quiet.

You were not to know who he was before?

Well, at first sight of him my focus was more on how nervous I was. He had a presence about him which told me he was not a person to mess around with. I guess, sort of like the bullies at school. Everybody knows to be careful around the bullies at school in case they are the next to fall victim to their violence or, worse, result as a friend who cannot serve their need. So, I then thought to myself it was most probably best to just keep quiet. Though, and as I am to know now, it is in quietness answers are to appear.

**Go on.**

Get up.

Me?

Stand up.

Me?

Look at yourself.

Me?

Go home, said the teacher.

I can't!

## Laugh at me.

My life had been flipped upside down and I was losing control fast. My sense of security, of comfort, of joy, of home had all gone. Gone so fast and I could do nothing. Nothing but accept it. Accept it! That is hard to do when you are only eight. Eight years old and you have gone from everything bad to everything even worse in the space of a single night, a single nightmare. I loved my father as much as I loved my mother and then I was to suddenly see my mother with another man. A man I did not really like.

My father was only around the corner but he might as well be gone because he was gone anyway. I did not see him. He did not see me. I had thought my father to be a complete coward. A coward for leaving us, a coward for trying to leave us and coward for not coming back for us. How could he not want to see his children and make sure they are okay when so much had happened and so much more was to come? Tell me, was I supposed to sit quietly and count to three? Close my eyes and count sheep?

## Laugh.

1. The man is not scared, for he has already been thrown into the deep long ago. The man, well known to those whom

have dared to mistake him, should not be remembered by true name but, instead, by true character.

## Do you

Bless whom has created this world, this universe in which we live, in which we reside alongside our humility and fortune, hate and forgiveness?

## Know

There is peace
In the birds which sing
And there is truth
In nature which grows
There is love
In our skies above
And there is more
Than we know down below

## Nothing?

It was not what I had wanted but it is what happened. He was now out of my life, my father. Since the time they'd divorced, my parents, I'd only seen him a handful of times before contact then stopped and he was gone.

Do you think that is what he had wanted?

## Wait.

2.

As he breathes in the air to feel the environment
He silently waits for a scratch to hear the squeak
While sitting in the darkness to hide from the light
He holds very gracefully a gun which kills the weak.

**Run.**

We have moved house once again. This house is to be my fifth house and it seems to be a whole lot better than the last already. The garden is the biggest garden I have ever seen, and we have talked frantically about the possibility of having so many good times together and starting over anew.

**Stop.**

Right behind our new house lay fields upon fields for as far as the eye could see, and it was the most beautiful way to escape after school had finished. There were many times often when my mother and I would take walks for hours on end with our little dog, and retreat to a place where it was just us, us in nature and nothing else. Yes, I have not yet mentioned it but we have just recently got a little dog and, he is the cutest, sweetest, most lovable thing ever, although I will speak more of him later. There were times when my mother and I would walk endlessly in silence and listen to the voices of the trees in the wind and the birds which sing within them, but then there were other times when we would instead talk about almost anything and pretty much everything until our hearts were filled, content.

There was this one time when my mother had wanted to tell me a lot, a lot of things about the past that in some way I think she had felt enormously guilty for. I can still remember standing with her by the barn and against the gate which looked out onto the fields we were both to admire most. She had started to explain why she was to divorce my father. I appreciated her honesty. It did sound as if she had a few second doubts though, as if it was actually the right thing to do. She had said there were no plans for the man to move in with us so soon, and it was only because he had no place to live that she tried to do what she thought best. She knew it was unfair. But, I guess, the hardest thing for her to tell me was what she had been keeping secret from my sister and I, about having almost died from cancer.

**Are you serious?**

Was it easier for her to say more about how she loved you both so much?

**It's all lies.**

Battling with cancer. She had been battling with cancer and until now I was not even to know. It had always been covered up. The lump on her neck. The loss of her hair. The days spent in bed. The times I had to go and stay at other houses. All of these things happened because she had cancer and I was not even to know. She could have died and I was not even to know! That is why they are not together any more. How selfish. How could it? How could he? My father. How could he have possibly been like that?

Stop it.

I do not even know if the cancer here is a blessing or a curse. Both, I guess. She had to have cancer to realise that she needed to live her life the way she wanted to. To do the things that she wanted to. To be who she wanted to be. The thing is, and I know I was young, and I know her intention was to protect us, I had not one idea about the way she had felt before. The way she had felt in her marriage. The way she had felt about herself. The way she felt about life. How was I to know when she had the biggest smile?

Stop it.

No. No matter how beautiful her smile was for everybody else, it was not for her. She was not the one to see the smile. She was living a life selflessly for him and what was she to get in return? All she wanted was to be appreciated. He had the sports car, the designer clothes, the expensive days out, the choices, the decisions, the control. He had the control over her. No, you cannot do that. No, we cannot go there. No. No. No. I know my mother could live without most things but she couldn't live without being herself.

## Does it matter?

Remind me how old you are?

Eleven

## Great.

It was a really great place where we had moved to. I had started a new school and made new friends, as well as keeping some older ones, which opened doors to experiencing new things. I had joined the local football team even though I had absolutely no idea how to play; I had joined the local drama group even though I had absolutely no idea how to act; I had joined in with all the local community events even though I had absolutely no idea who anyone was; and I had even started to accept the involvement of the man my mother was so fond of. He wasn't so bad really.

The village became something like a family to me. It built me up when I was knocked down; it provided me direction when I was lost; it cared for me at a time when I cared not too much for myself but was too much responsibility to place upon only one, and it had given me the opportunity to feel as if I really belonged to something more. I could see that everybody in the community was always willing to help one another and usually without expectation; I could see that everybody was wanting to give rather than thinking to receive, and I really, seriously, needed to be a part of that.

**Whatever.**

Together is always better.

**It will not last.**

Wow, I remember this one garden party we had. It must have stood out for miles, and I mean miles, because there, in the middle, we had the most enormous fire. Hundreds of people from the village had come to celebrate with us, and each of them thoughtfully contributed something wonderfully temptatious to share. There actually happened to be so much for everybody to enjoy, it was almost too much, but then who is really to say such things?

I remember at the party when the people were singing and dancing to the music playing, laughing and giggling to the children fooling, falling into a memorable romance when time took a sudden still, and I remember, when we ignited that fire of ours, the fireworks shot taller than the starlit night sky high up above. We were certainly very fortunate to have so many people come into our lives and to have such a beautiful place to call home.

**Don't.**

3. Although the man has a weakness and he cannot stand weakness for the same reason he cannot stand fear, it induces an inward rage to that of a bird in a cage, and he is a great admirer of birds and how they can fly...

**What?**

Please forgive me.

**You're mad.**

Will there ever be a time when we can all put the guns down? Not just guns but any given weapon that has the potential to take somebody out from their being, their existence here, unnecessarily. It is easy to say that one has the choice to fight but how about the one who doesn't? What about the poor? The uneducated? The hungry? The desperate?

Money bets the one who has a choice is not the one out there fighting, they are not the one in view of blame but are to blame, if we were to blame.

Those who fight are not my enemies but are my friends. They are my friends yet they know not. I may not salute what they do but I do appreciate them for who they are. For if they were not to be victims under a past of gluttony and avarice, of neglect and disrespect then it would not be guns they carry but gifts they shared with us instead. They are people.

I say this because I happened to fall victim of a gun recently. I do not remember much in the hell and blurriness other than this simple thought:

Why do we continue to live in a world of madness when it does not cost the earth to change? To not change is actually and only at the cost of us.

**Stupid?**

I think selfishness tops the hierarchy or stupidity. What about jealousy?

What is the difference between selfishness and jealousy?

**Do it.**

4.

His finger slowly reaches out to pull back the trigger
The trigger held responsible for a many of those dead
When we are only to watch weak in our slavery
Bless the small innocent rodent lifting up his little head.

# Chapter Three

**Get real.**

Imagine standing by the remains of a fire, still smouldering, and trying not to inhale what would damage, if not kill, you though you could not walk away. You could only turn your back and then only for a moment before the smoke would once again find you, play with you and then choke you, take you. Imagine, if you will, standing in the chains of death: in the chains of life.

**I can't.**

The years go by. They go so fast. Is it just you as I? Are we to last?

**I don't know.**

I didn't really like him before and then it all happened to change. It happened to change when he started taking me to the bar to meet his friends and the people he knew from around town. It seemed to be an all right place to go, I guess. Everybody went there. They all seemed to have a good time and it was friendly enough. I did find it interesting how the people would talk about things which were not usually said back at home though. Things which, I thought, probably should be said back at home. The man often said many things. He would, at times, become so passionate in his expression that he was able to make us believe in anything he said.

I did think to myself, for a moment, why it was easier to talk there than anywhere else. Was it like those who go to a priest to confess their sins and after doing so they are supposed to feel much better? Or, perhaps, similar to those who write down their thoughts in diaries, instead of telling them to the ones they have in mind, and then hoping for the best without really doing anything? I don't know. Although, what I did like was the sense of togetherness the bar had with the people. There were nights when I would sit there and listen for hours, to all of their problems, and I was to learn an awful lot from them but never why they had wanted to drink so much.

**Yeah.**

I had better wake up for school in the morning.

**He didn't care.**

It wasn't fair but he didn't care because he ended up having exactly what he wanted and he wanted everything which left us with, well, nothing…

**Yeah?**

Again. Again, we have to move. Do you know why we have to keep on moving, God? I think I know. God, do you think you can understand me?

**Rubbish.**

There was nothing left to it. Love had gone. Hope had vanished. Just like that. The house felt like it had turned into nothing but a hollow box furnished with uncertainty. Nobody wanted to be there. The man would usually be found at the bar and I would usually be found with friends after school finding trouble, finding some way to escape. For my sister she, I hate to say it, was usually alone. She was usually alone because she didn't have anybody else, she only had our mother, and Mother couldn't be there.

### Listen.

What do you think makes a man? Today, we are packing up our things to go. To leave this place we all love so much. To go to some other place none of us want to go. Although, we have to. There is no other place for us now.

### Let it happen.

Since my mother left my father, we've had next to no money to get by and the man didn't make matters any better either. Actually, he only made things more difficult, to be honest. These are the kinds of discussions my mother and I had on our walks together. What kind of situation had she put us in? Should she be the one to blame when we struggled to put food on the table? Was she the one to blame when everybody was left feeling unhappy and unwanted and angry and frustrated? And I said to her, no.

No way was she to blame. I did find it hard to understand why she had cheated on my father and, after so many years of knowing him, why she could not have been more honest. Why did she have to go behind his back? And, I asked her one time if she thought it would have been possible to resolve the issues, had they been able to talk to one another properly, and she didn't really answer me as such. She had a certain way of telling me the truth by looking into my eyes and letting me trust my own thoughts.

**You're quite right.**

Awakened eyes will always see. That is what you have told me.

**I had no idea.**

You see, there is a lot about the man that I did not know. I had first judged him on what he was rather than who he was but now, over the past couple of years of living with him, I have come to see him in a different shade of light. That is not to say he is what he is not, he can certainly be a complete and utter intolerant person at times, but the man has the biggest heart and something within him I am only left totally affected and honoured to know it so. The problem is he was locked out. His parents had stolen his keys when he was only a child and never did give them back. They either never thought to give them back or they couldn't. As my thoughts wonder, it may be the parents had no idea whatsoever, they didn't know of any such keys. It could also be the parents once had their keys stolen and, without ever intending to, they did the same, not being able to prevent the pain and poor suffering. I am not to say which and, regardless of my thoughts, I could see it was only to leave the man in a torn state of dying love and living hate, and this was often demonstrated upon the others he appreciated most. I was a witness to his actions all of the time and I would get caught up in the emotional debris it left, swept across the people and places closest to me. There were times when I could not understand why he would do such things, inflict so much pain and anger upon others, provoke evil to rise out from the kind-hearted and bad from those who did good. Was it fair? Then I was to know he ran away from home as a child. I was to learn he was beaten many times. Whipped. Smacked. Hit. Embarrassed. Unloved. His parents, other than doings these things, more or less, ignored him, neglected him, rejected him. Treated him in a way so he thought it was best to run away, aged at sixteen. He had thought to himself that he would stand a better chance alone than to be around those who acted as if they hated his being. He tried to run as far as it was possible, with the hope that somehow the pain that he had would be left behind somewhere other than...

### Here, was it you?

'What are you doing around here? I didn't know you live around here.'

'I've only just moved here. What are you doing around here?'

'Nothing much.'

'Oh, right.' I could see through the darkness he was not alone.

'Where do you live?'

'A couple of blocks that way.'

'Right.'

'What about you? Don't you live the other side of here?' There were now a few of them on his side, all staring at me. 'I have to get going.'

'Why don't you stay?'

I have to go.

'No, you don't.'

I could sense that they wanted some kind of trouble. 'Look, I am going.' I turned around to walk away as one of them started to cross the road.

'Wait here.'

My heart had started to pound a little heavy.

'Come here.' Somebody had shouted louder.

As I turned, two hands suddenly wrapped around my neck.

'I have you, boy. You'd better start praying.'

His hands were squeezing so hard I couldn't breathe. He wasn't letting go and my feet couldn't touch the ground.

## I hate you.

It is not fair, God! It is not fair! Why is she the one to suffer such pain? Why has it come back? God? Why? Why has the cancer come back? Tell me! Do you think she is the one to deserve this? Do you? Tell me! God?

## My dearest.

They were basically inseparable most of the time, my sister and mother. My sister, for the first two years of her life, had to fight for her life. There was uncertainty whether or not she would be able to live, to survive the implications that she had been challenged with when born. Most of her days were spent in and out of hospital, most of her days were spent not knowing, just wanting to live. To live life and to love. To know love and to have a chance to spend time with a mother who knew nothing else other.

## Tell me.

Love, is there such a thing?

There is nothing more real than love.

And pain?

Yes, that is real too, my son. Yet, I say this, love as much as you can.

Forget the pain, just love?

## Do you believe?

Sometimes, you have to ride blind into the darkness. Sometimes, you have to drive straight into your fears. Sometimes, you have to do what's wrong from right. Sometimes, you have to bow down to the devil which appears.

Sometimes, you'll have to go loose on the run. Sometimes, you'll have to sleep lonely on the street. Sometimes, you'll have to fight those you love most. Sometimes, you'll have to taste the experience of what is bittersweet.

Sometimes, you have to find out the reasons why. Sometimes, you have to live, let go, and forget. Sometimes, you have to pretend you're somebody you're not. Sometimes, you have to live your life free and without regret.

## I know him.

It was as the raucous sound approached closer that the man had just about taken enough of the commotion and decided to act out what he thought best. As he stood up from his bar stool, he slammed down hard his drink on the side with half of its contents spilling out onto the floor before angrily storming his way over to the door, without fear, and ignoring the voices. The voices of those who knew him well, who had said to him to just calm down and shouted aloud that it was not worth it and, if he was to do anything, it will only make matters ten times worse. But I knew, as did they, that was not his concern at this moment in time because when the man had a problem, there was going to be a problem and so much more.

The man headed straight outside the front to confront whatever, or whoever, it was creating such a sound so horrible, that it soured bitter the faces of those drinking among him. A sound so ridiculous that it was an embarrassment to acknowledge the presence of such obscenity in such a place at such a time. We were, after all, only having a lunchtime pint. Yet it was then, when the man marched outside, straight into the road which passed the bar and without care nor hesitation, forced a speeding car to a sudden stop — the man waved his arms around like a frank lunatic dancing on an old-fashioned spinning top, and pointing to the other guy to get out and fight. He was to become somebody, I knew he was not.

## Like I know cancer.

Not many times could we go and spend time with our mother while she was in hospital. She was isolated for her chemotherapy and if she wasn't receiving the treatment, she was most often too weak, or too uncomfortable, to accept us as visitors. It was not that she didn't want to see us but more that she didn't want us to see her in the condition she was in; my mother was noted to be a rather beautiful woman and, though she was regularly acknowledged for her looks, elegance and grace, she was never one to be shadowed in vanity or to think of herself in great confidence either. And, with the ever-changing effects of the cancer she had been battling, her image was to radically alter and her confidence, at first, was to be reduced to almost nothing, if anything, at all. Which leaves importance to the point I make when talking of beauty: I hope for it to be thought in both what is and what isn't seen. It was easy to see the fading and the changing happening on the outside, the things that we had to learn, understand and accept as different to that we had loved before, yet what was to be the biggest change, the most surreal change, for me is that it didn't separate my mother and I but instead allowed us to recognise each other, which cannot be forgotten.

**He said.**

Is it within hope and faith to which makes us feel most alive?

**Burn baby.**

I had to lie. I don't think I had lied for him. I think I had lied for her. My mother. To the police. I lied. I lied and she cried. And he was still arrested. Eight police men and two dogs it took to get the man down on the floor and handcuffed. I was surprised not to see him beat them up more than he did.

'Burn baby burn' are the words I remember. 'Burn in hell'. It is not a very nice thing to say to a family, is it? Especially after telling them to go back to their own country. I was with the man when he had said it. I know he had meant it. He hated foreigners but I didn't want my mother to find out.

**Exactly.**

Is it fair to throw your emotion onto another?
Your anger to a brother?
Your frustration to a sister?
Your hate to a father?
Your need to a mother?
Is it not fair to live life exactly how you feel?

**Pause.**

He furiously slams on the brakes of the car and gets out into the middle of the road during the rush-hour when the traffic is mayhem. He walks without care over to the other vehicle, the vehicle that had two seconds ago, cut us up and almost caused us to crash, and heads directly towards the driver's window. Various cars are swerving, skewing, to avoid hitting him, but it doesn't look like he takes much notice, he doesn't even flinch and his fists are clenched tight. As the window of the other vehicle is closed, he starts screaming at the guy to wind it down. The guy is reluctant, he doesn't do it, his face now giving the impression that he has just confronted somebody who he cannot match and his stupid, stupid-looking piece of shit car is just a little bit out of place. Everybody is stopping, or has already stopped to watch, and the road is now in chaos while I am sitting down quite comfortably in the passenger seat of our car — with a front row view I could be doing worse. The guy still has not wound down his window and it looks like he is trying to apologise through the glass. However, it's really not working for him. The tension is becoming extraordinary and the outcome is now, more or less, inevitable. The guy slowly winds his window down and at the same time, the man's fist thumps through to knock his face a fair distance left, and then totally out.

### This isn't his fault!

He was an influence
Perhaps not the greatest one but he was an influence
A small-town mind with a big-time mouth
A patriot of his country without any true purpose
A hater to those he decided not to like
Homophobic
Racist
Classist
Sexist
And judged those he thought dumb
But none of this was ever his fault

**Breathe.**

Have you ever considered what it would be like to drown?

To lose your breath not knowing whether you will ever get it back?

To fall endlessly, yet still able to see the last glimmering flicker of light?

To enter into a distance, a distance that not even I could go?

Welcome home.


**Surrender.**

Vodka, gin, whiskey and rum. Until the end of the bottle I am not done. Fifteen years old and out.

Get it? Stuck. Surrounded by nothing but feculence, I had wanted to drink. God — to my wistful escape.

Why is the Vitruvian Man the last thing I see before spinning down into the depths of hell and pleading to who or what it is that I am to call God?

It was four or five o'clock in the morning and I had woken up in severe panic as my heart beat six feet from out of my chest, and I was to have absolutely no idea where I was. I did not even know what was real. I could see to my left side that I had been attached to a drip and I could see underneath the sheet that all my clothes had been removed, but I could not remember anything, nothing, except for the experience which had woken me. Confused though I was, I had asked the nurse what happened and she said, in a way to make me feel worse, that I had been brought to the hospital by an ambulance that a friend had called; that I had drowned myself unconscious with alcohol; and that I had been out cold for hours.

But pleading to God? Spiralling down to hell as the

Vitruvian Man?

At first, I was the man, positioned like him for sure and turning in a clockwise movement looking upwards. Then, a darkness came over me. I dropped suddenly into, what seemed like, a never-ending descent leaving behind something I can't quite describe. I remember feeling this enormous weight of guilt pulling me down as I started to become aware of what I had done, but I was only trying to forget that my mother was ill. In desperation, I started to promise and plead to God that I had done wrong, that I wouldn't do it again though the flames had already started to burn beneath my back and I could begin to hear the devil laughing. It was only in my last thoughts that I'd managed to project out from the fall. Da Vinci?

I remember being forgiven but it was only by voice, no image. I was weak and helpless. I was completely weak and helpless.

# Chapter Four

**Never.**

If I had never gone, if I had never been given the chance, I wonder how different everything would be. Would I be able to see in the ways that I do now, think in the ways that I do now? Would I be here, who I am or even feel the ways that I feel? I wonder, if I had never gone, if I would be able to understand, if I would be as passionate, would I love in the ways that I do? And I wonder, and I only wonder, if it could have been any other way?

**You know.**

There was a lot to learn this year, my fifteenth year, ten years ago. You are already to know my mother had been battling cancer, that she had spent the majority of her time in hospital receiving chemotherapy treatment and you are already to know the destructive impact the cancer then led to spread throughout our lives at home and how we had come to fall apart without her being there for us. You are already to know the man was not capable of looking after anyone else other than himself and, even then, he was not able to do that very well, and you are already to know, a little, about the needs of my sister and how she was very much dependent on the help of somebody who was willing to give her the time, the love necessary.

You are already to know that I was starting to fall back, to fall behind at school and not only was I stepping outside of the norm there, the accepted, but also in all other social circles and environments that I had managed to become involved with over the last few years, and you are already to know that I was not to be kept very well hidden from the presence of violence and absurdity, of hatred and abuse directed towards others either. You are already to know, or perhaps not know but instead think, that a continuation in ways, and ways similar, will only lead me to a place far and much worse than where I am already to be, but what you are not already to know is that something had the possibility to change everything.

**I'm so lucky.**

It is as dangerous as it is beautiful but it is Africa, and it is alive and it is the place I had been given the opportunity to go and visit with my school.

You had been given the opportunity to go to Africa?

It was the best thing that could have happened to me at the time. This lady had wanted to try and establish a connection between the secondary school I was attending and a secondary school in the heart of Uganda. When it was confirmed, talks were in progress, everybody had the chance to be one of the first representatives of our school and, hopefully, get to go out there.

And the school had chosen you as one of the representatives?

Yes! They had chosen me as one of the eleven or twelve students and not only was I to have this, what they had called, 'life-changing experience', but I was also able to share it with two of my best friends at the time. I could not honestly believe, and most definitely did not realise until we were able to go, how valuable, how important, this event was going to be.

And what do you mean by valuable and important?

With everything going on back at home, and not that many people knew of it, there were times when I really thought to myself what was I going to do? What would I do if I was no longer to have my mother around to help me, if I was to be surrounded by the things I did not like and to get caught up with bad people, to lose hope, or to give up on hope in life and at school?

And how did having this experience change these thoughts for you?

Because when I was to get out there, 'in the heart which is life', I knew I was not alone. Something happened to me. I had felt, in what I call, God.

## Why?

I haven't said much about my sister yet because I find it enormously difficult to. Difficulty is the main constituent of our relationship, between my sister and I, and until this present day I still struggle to express what she means to me and how I think of her. I guess, to put it simply, she is 'perfect', we all are, yet there is so much more to say about her than that.

As I have briefly mentioned before, she almost didn't make survival past two years of age and even with her willingness to, and want for life, she has had to strive over defect and illness time and time again. Making friends was hard for her, nobody was to understand her, give time to get to know her and growing up I was to be a part of this unfair thoughtlessness.

It is not because I wanted to be either, I just didn't know

another way how. We were to be brought up together with no differences and with the same chances; I was not even to know properly why it was that my sister had to go to a school different to me. It was unfortunate, really, this principle was to falter when I had started to become aware of our distinctive disparities.

It was easy for me to make many friends; it was easy for me to attend school and do well; it was easy for me to go and do whatever it was that captured my curiosity; it was easy for me to be active and healthy and to join in with all the others; it was easy for me to thrive on things which made me happy. It was not easy to know my sister could not do the same.

### I am going to cry.

We had only been there a few days before the phone call. We were already to have experienced things I did not believe as real because I could never, in all my classes, imagine such life to be in ways now seen. With all my appreciation of thought, it took a little time to regard it in mind but it was not that I had seen which held most impact here, more what I heard…

### Bless you.

A few months earlier and after a long confrontation with the cancer she had been challenged with, our mother was to receive the best news any person suffering such torment can wish for: the all-clear. She had done it. She had managed to beat the cancer once again and to see us and to smile like she did was the proudest, the strongest thing I have yet to experience.

It had been a hard time without her, for all of us. She was

47

our eminence and our guidance, she was our light and our hope and without her there, with us, there was no us. We were torn apart, ripped up, split up — done. As I've already said, the man was big enough and ugly enough to look after himself although he failed to do so. And as for my sister, I am so, so sorry…

**Mother.**

'Mum?'

'Yes, Son.'

'How are you?'

'I am okay, how are you?'

'I am great thanks, Mum.'

'How are you finding it there?'

'It is amazing, I have so much to tell you…'

'Mum?'

'Yes, Son?'

'Are you okay? Please, tell me you are okay?'

'Mum?'

'I did not want you to find out this way.

'No, no, no.'

'It has come back. I am so sorry, Son.'

**Please.**

Before the storm of my devilish ways, I pray for thee.

**All that is beautiful.**

The little boat floats upon a lake in Africa and, although small in size, she is most certainly almighty in character and plenty extraordinary in experience. She fears not the swarming beasts of nature which lay below her, nor the weathers which greet her from above and it is said, throughout her younger days of innocent youth, she was as delicate as a raindrop painted upon a bright white lily, and it is clear, when the sun shines the sky pretty, to see her beauty still holding patina as old petals wilt and new rain falls. Though, it is unfortunate, in all her celebration, she is broken.

Taken from her years and time again, man has been trying every way imaginable to save her in his heroics. For all his own self-doubt and fear, he has impacted upon her nature, her gifted way of life and to the eyes which see, who have seen her for that she really is, comprehension to man's thought is nothing difficult to understand. Man, here, has captured her as possession. He has claimed ownership and responsibility for all her power, image and worth, anchoring any such appreciation to nothing less than simple, mere objectification. Man, here, has chosen force over truth.

He is not yet to realise that it is he already in her possession, life, and to catch this in sail is how to stand free. The water around her dances, glistens to the light and the show is nothing less than a reflection of the wonders I stare to above. The endless giving joy itself, myself, I am sure could go on somewhere, here and there, forever though I am to stand with her in the midst of this calm, waiting for God, waiting to be baptised by nature. She knew, when blues turned into greys and cooler breezes of air swept away the last rays of sun, I was never to believe I could be alone, even if I was…

Lashes of good rain began to strike down hard across my face and athwart my back whilst a laughing of thunder hailed in excitement over me. The waters turned into what was not to shine but throw us from side to side and away from safety and close enough to see into the widening jaws of the great hippopotamuses and the crocodiles, which had moved and crept their way across the stormy waters. It was only then, and only in rhythm, the tempest rapidly pervaded the scene with an abundance of passion; nature, in all her might and her majesty, had trusted her secrets upon me.

**Save me.**

It is in her spirit which keeps me above.

**I can't.**

It was her that used to look after me, now it is me that has to look after her. Her illness has taken over the physical body and no longer can she go very far without the need of a wheelchair, nor can she breathe properly without the aid of an apparatus. She has, once again, lost all of her long flowing hair and, with the cancer now spreading out everywhere and fast, it has rapidly taken over and captured the entirety of her appearance and ability of life.

**You'll be okay.**

School wasn't really working out very well for me again. I had lost interest in that I was being taught, in what I was being told to do and say and how to act and how to dress and what is right and what is wrong and just how everything should be but isn't and isn't because it is wrong and not right. I was fed up with it. I was much more concerned with everything else, everything that was taking place back at home and how it may really take effect on my life and, if it was to, what am I to do? Who am I to be then?

It was only because I had to go to school that I still went to school and, even though I was there, I was then to spend most of my time outside of the classroom rather than inside, as I was now considered to be somewhat of a bad influence. I was considered to be disruptive and a disadvantage upon the others and it all started to make better sense, as I stood outside with nothing to do, that it was much easier for them to send me outside to mind my own thoughts than to be allowed in and be myself amongst everyone.

**Be yourself.**

All I am is just an expression of my experience.

**Always.**

The door opened and in came my mother crying. She had just returned from the hospital. I can remember it in every detail. It all happened so slowly. She had her head placed down into hands, hiding the eyes which cried so painfully. Then, she looked up and ran over to me. She put her arms around me. Hugged me. It felt like she never wanted to let go of me.

Nothing was to be said for a while. I didn't want anything to be said. I was already to know. Sometimes you are just all ready to know. She had been told that she had only six weeks left. To live. She had been told that she had only six weeks left to live. Though, she said, she had come to accept death. This life, what she cared for most, were the lives of her children.

In tears, I had told her that she was so very brave and there was nothing to be worried about. I said, 'I will do everything I can to look after my sister and as for myself, well, you know me.' Her tears, which she cried so sadly, suddenly turned into those of laughter, as did mine, and together we cherished that which we had. And as I write this, we very much still have.

**It's true.**

Did you really run into a hippopotamus?
Yes!
It is strange what can stand in the way, isn't it?

**Celebrate.**

We had gone to a party, our, what you are supposed to call, family and one of my closer friends who happened to live nearby. We were to celebrate an occasion with the people of the village down in the hall where there was music, entertainment and, with that, drunken dancing to be seen by none, but all. Everybody looked to be having such a great time, as the food was good and the wine was fine, though some said the beer was much better and, with that, they had another and another, until the bar had no other, except vodka, gin, whiskey and rum and that is when I thought to have some. Not from the bar, of course, but rather from the table when I was able to get away, leaving nothing to say, from the adults who were talking of my adolescence which they had been watching. Now I am fifteen and I have been through quite a lot, and not once forgot how I was to feel in some of the experiences I have already had, remembering I was not to have a dad to look up to, only a mother, who was dying, and nobody was to see when I was crying out for somebody to save her and stop this pain, this torture but no, God? There is no God. I am just crazy to believe in what is, at best, only a fragment of all my wildest thoughts... Wait, one moment, wait, here comes the man. Please, pause here, please...

**Relax.**

And without them knowing how, the man had knocked him unconscious.

**Love.**

> In your mind
> You burst out
> Screaming
> Mind explosions
> Your neurons
> Bleeding
> Listen to the voices
> Speaking
> Is it not
> Your heart
> Which is calling?

**I love you.**

I remember she was sitting at the dining room table as I was to look into the mirror ahead of her. Her hair was now short, grey and fuzzy, and the apparatus was now constantly attached over her nose. She was sitting there alone, waiting for us to join her. She could hardly move any more. I don't know if she knew, at the time, if I was looking but she suddenly gave a little smile. It was so peaceful to know that, through all the pain she was experiencing, she still had just enough strength and spirit to show her true self. She was, if nothing else, a smile of God which lighted upon my heart.

**I will be there for you.**

What is it for a boy to watch a man give second breath to his mother and then take her life?

Any closer and I would have killed him. I am sure of it. I wouldn't have given it a second thought. We were in the kitchen at the time and there were several items that could have done him fatal, but the way my blood boiled inside I would have taken him with the bare of my own two hands.

What are you to do when your mother teaches you the real meaning of life and you are yet to understand?

I remember as he martialled through the back door, stinking of beer and cigarettes. He shouted, 'Where the fuck were you? Who do you think you are, woman? You make me sick.' He got right up into my mother's face as her head bowed downward, afraid, and her body shivered, scared to death.

He acted like a monster with saliva spitting out from his dry, souring mouth. His back was hunched over, beast-like, and his finger pointed towards her as if it was a rusted blunt knife ready to kill. It looked like he was capable as he continued to pour out all of his anger, all of his evil.

What would have been if my mother hadn't blessed me in her spirit and guidance long before the hour of light?

I fell in-between that of quiet love and thunderous hate. I pushed the man away from my mother, hoping not to get hit as the tears rolled slowly down the side of my face. He swayed and swerved carelessly into the living room, portraying not even a sign of sin or a flicker of consciousness in his being.

# Chapter Five

**Believe in me.**

I am talking to you. Who are you talking to? You. Me? I am confused, me? Am I the one listening or am I the one talking? Listening. No, talking. Now I don't know. You always do this. Why can it never be simple? It is simple. No, it isn't. Who is the one talking? Me. And who is the one listening? You.

**Have hope.**

Don't be afraid
She told me
Your journey
Is guided
By the light
Of angels
Whom rest by
Your darkest side

**Lose hope.**

Early one morning in January, the man came into my room and said to me my mother had gone. She had passed away in the middle of the night.

**Nothing is half of what is.**

I saw her there

Laying there, still
I had gone into the room on my own
I had wanted to say goodbye
I had wanted to show my respect
Though, as I was to stand ahead
In front of her
I was to feel nothing
Who was lying there
In front of me
Was not my mother
Yes, it was her body
The way her body was to look after the cancer
Though, as I was to sit by her side
Holding her hand
I was to feel nothing
And I thought
For a while
She really must have gone to some other place
Or to no place at all and how I am to be left here
Alone and without her
Though, I wasn't
I was not, nor could be, alone
I was only not to understand what nothing really is

**Be scared.**

Nightmares, if continued in dream, will become reality.
Wake up. Wake up. But my eyes are not closed, the day is not
yet night. Wake up. Wake up!

**Laugh at yourself.**

There are no ways to say goodbye properly

There are no places we both cannot go
There are no words which we can say
To explain all the things that we know

## Go out and be alone.

I would go out each night to wander the streets which were left soulless. Where the moon would see sympathy, creating friends for me in the shadows of a time when the air would pass by like a spirited blessing for the cleansing of my soul. I remember being so angry, so upset. I had wanted to hide all of the people who surrounded me from the way I was feeling. They were only to see me strong, that is what I had told myself. To see me managing, to see me coping with the loss of my mother, and to see me looking after my sister being the brave brother, I had once before promised.

I thought to myself if there was anyone I could turn to, to be honest with. I was angry at God, or who I had wanted God to be. I forever had such a strong belief that everything was going to be okay, that everything only happened for a reason and that everything would eventually turn out for the better. Before I would try to picture an image in mind of my family sitting in the sun by the waters of the sea, with nothing to worry about and able, allowed, to be me. Though, that was nothing other than a joke as I would go out each night to wander the streets which were left soulless.

## Try to understand.

Love is so delicate
Like the falling
Of a snowflake
On a sun-kissed

Winters day
Caught
In a calming wind
Which passes by
To wish hope
Upon your rosy-cold face
Sent down from above
Formed in total purity
And perfection
A snowflake dances freely
Without worry
For it does not know
Time
Other than now
To enjoy which it has
To give
The truest most reflective image
So, troubled I am
To know
Such things cannot last
Forever
Only in my dearest appreciation
When touched by beauty
And to know the blessed
And to know the loved
Is so delicate

**Try to think of others.**

Even though the man was a total bully I was still to feel
sorry for him. Foolish? I know. My mother was the same. But
it was not possible to walk away. Not then. That would have

concluded in failure. I would have failed him. The man was a helpless case. So it seemed. Riddled in depression and covered in hate, the man needed help. My help. He was no longer to have my mother and who else would have taken such chances? Who else would have given their life? I did not know of anyone who would have.

I had been told I had chances to go and my sister would have followed me wherever I thought best, but my decision was to stay. Stay with the man and see what I can do to try and make this awful situation just a little better for all of us. Not just me. Not just my sister. But had I known better, never would I have made such a decision. Never would I have put my sister through this tragic torment, though it was not possible for me to walk away. Not then. That would have concluded in failure. I would've failed.

## You are allowed to be angry.

I have just come to learn that during the time my mother was going through her second and third battles with cancer, a time when she had worried herself even sicker with the thought of how my sister and I would be able to afford to get by, live, with the little money we had and her no longer being able to work, that my father had been building his own house. His own fucking house while we were living on a council estate.

See, I was to learn much earlier on, when on walks with my mother, that when they had divorced, he, my father, had placed down a quick get-out-and-go offer to her to foresee, to prevent, any further complications — or closer to the case, fairness — later on down the line, if in court. And knowing my mother — soft, not worthy, and more importantly then, desperate — he gave her a sum not even ten percent of what would have been an equal share.

Both my parents acted weak in many senses but my mother especially in the case of not allowing herself to have what she deserved, that she deserved without consequence. She neither had great forethought as her inability to not allow herself to have what she deserved prevented it also for others, mainly my sister and I. I am not to lay blame here on my mother either, more on my father's greed and utter selfishness, even if he had been hurt.

When taking the money my mother knew she was making the wrong decision, though she did not know of another way to solve it and her ever-growing guilt for leaving and cheating on my father, was to be her way of telling herself that it was fair, that it was right to accept his offer and leave the past behind. Yet, that was never going to be the case in the way that if she actually knew him. The man she had gone running to, to try and start anew.

**Just please be careful.**

Tell me why she never got to have what she deserved?

How do you know that she did not?

Look at the way she was treated by the people in her life.

How well did you know your mother?

I would say really well.

And are you sure of that?

Yes.

I would question it.

Why would you question it?

You had only been a part of her life for fifteen years.

We had talked about many things that had happened

before.

Most of those fifteen years you were only a child.

Still, I would say that I knew my mother really well.

I am not saying that you did not.

Then what are you trying to say?

I am trying to help you understand that which you questioned.

Are you telling me that she did get what she deserved?

I am only saying how well did you really know your mother?

## Let the pain flow through.

In my spaces of weakness, he had hurt me like the kind of pain that kills peace. Only two, maybe three, months had gone by since our mother passed and the man called me one morning to ask if we could talk about a couple of things which became of sudden importance. It was during these months the man had not been at the house, he had left my sister and I to go and work away in London, and although it may scream out abandonment, I am glad that he had because he was known very well to fall into very serious and deep bouts of depression. He would, in some cases, remain for weeks lying asleep downstairs so, for me, it was most definitely a good thing to see him trying to do something for himself and to, as well, earn.

Money was a real issue for us. Obviously, our mother had nothing to leave in inheritance and the benefits the man received as our now 'guardian' reduced at the same time we had been given a notice to leave the property we had been renting. It was only a matter of time before we were going to have to move again and where to, I only dreaded to think. It was rare to find available properties for poor people in the area we lived. With this in mind I only hoped that whatever the man had to tell was nothing more serious than all that we had been going through hitherto though what was I to expect? Almost anything but this. The man turned to me and said, 'Please don't take this the wrong way but I have found somebody else now.'

## You will be strong.

'Get in the car.'

'You've been drinking.'

'Get in the car.'

'We're not getting in the car.'

'Stop being so stupid.'

'I promised them I wouldn't let you drive us drunk.'

'I am not drunk.'

'You've had enough not to drive.'

'Just get in the car.'

'No.'

'Why are you being like this?'

'Me?'

'Yes, who else?'

'Just leave it.'

'Have it your way.'

'Where is my sister?'

'Already in the car.'

'Wait!'

## I'll try my best.

I ran after the man to try and stop him though he turned to me with his fists clenched in rage and, for a moment, I thought I was going to be the next person to get his punch, but he

hesitated to hit me and whilst in shock I had instead waited for
him to take the door and slam it against my face hard enough
to knock me down onto the floor and for him to walk before I
could get back up onto my feet and stop him driving off drunk.

## You will stand up.

And if you stumble, make sure not to fall.

## You will see a light.

Not only had the man gone and found somebody else now,
he had also come to tell me that he may have cancer. What was
he possibly thinking? Did he really think I was going to
sympathise with him? That I would be understanding of his
needs for another woman because he cannot handle life
himself? Did he really think that he had cancer and, I am sorry
to say this, even if he did, did he not think to keep it to himself
or at least away from me until he was absolutely certain of the
truth in the matter of this subject? Why did it always have to
be about him and why was he always so utterly selfish and
completely ignorant to everybody else who was there and
around to help him? Who had said to him, time and time again,
'we are there for you, we will help you.' Yet, he was still to put
up his giant brick wall of defence and shut them out because
so far down his life had been he could trust no other to actually,
actually help him and the next best thing he could do, and as
he has always done, was to find somebody else in which he
could control to make up for it. An effort he would go to, to try
and gain a sense of power over himself by using others in the
form of puppetry and by then forcing, manipulating their
emotions to best suit his.

**You will see you.**

True colours, what are your true colours? What do you think are mine?

I can remember listening to the school children in Uganda singing the lyrics to one of my childhood favourite songs, being so because it was also one of my mother's. Not one of her childhood favourites of course, she was born in sixty-one and I in ninety-two, but one because, she said, she connected within it the sound of hope and the notion of self-love through the gifts of another and like the school children in Uganda and all over...

**You will feel God.**

There has been left an imprint upon my heart like a melodic calling from God wishing me to come back home. How on earth do I ever get to go home?

**You may not want to.**

The house was now always a mess, dirty and untidy, things scattered the floors in all directions being left to grow old and/or, completely forgotten altogether. The smoke was now to fill the rooms in a cloudy grey and, with no windows left open to extract the smell of death from under our noses, the rain bashed hard against the glass panes leaving no colour in either of our lives in any direction. The man laid down his body to rest on the sofa, again most days, as I attempted school though at times it was too much and I had skipped out of the lessons I could get away with and not be noticed. The atmosphere at 'home', it was no longer home, was vile enough to make me feel sick, and it reeked a stench strong enough to kill even the ugliest of rodents who scratch down to the bare existence of whatever life they may have in the dark and dirt beneath us. I had always tried to clean up the house whenever I could, yet it was a completely pointless and hopeless case.

Neither was there to be any appreciation of me doing it but the man would also turn the place back into a slum within hours and I grew ever so tired of cleaning, fixing up after him and his foul behaviour and his attitude towards me and having to tell myself afterwards that everything will be okay and to breathe in and to calm down. 'No!' He was out one day, I don't know where, I never did, and I was sorting through some things in a hopeful attempt to uncover a sense of comfort within the house again, and I was to find these letters among the piles of rubbish. They were letters on headed paper depicting the logo of the police department. There, on the letters, it read out the cause of a criminal act perpetrated by the man and furthermore backed up with clear evidence. There, I saw, he had smashed up the local shop something crazy, in a violent rage on Valentine's Day. For a very good reason why he really did not want to say.

### Don't give up.

This isn't easy, believe me. I can't stop going back. I can't stop thinking what everything means. I can't stop thinking if it means anything at all.

What is the point, really? We go through so much pain, so much suffering and most of the time it seems like there is no reason for it, no real purpose.

There is no happy ending, at least not for everybody. I see some people are fortunate and some are blessed but then I see some people are to be nothing.

What is it for somebody to live and never have the chance

to live as them? To live a life of another, too afraid to go out alone for a life of their truth.

**I know I have.**

Have you ever considered the real feeling of failure, the feeling of not following your heart far enough to believe the difference of you is exactly the amount needed in our world for everything to equal what we can't all see but is perfect? I know I have, so often. I know exactly how failure feels.

I had returned home one day to find out my sister was not there. She would always be there, in her room. I had called her phone several times but I was to get no answer. I had kept on trying, friends, family, nothing. Hours passed, nothing. The night passed, nothing. I was to wake up, hoping.

Nothing. I had told myself she must have gone to a friend's house to stay. I had thought to myself that in her loneliness she may have gone and done something stupid. I had told myself it was all my fault. It was me who had abandoned her. I had thought to myself it was me who had let her down.

If only I was to think of her instead of myself throughout this time past. I had promised our mother I would take care of her and what have I done but let her down. She needed me. I was hardly ever there. 'No, don't think like that. She must have just gone to stay at a friend's house. She'll call.'

I was not to hear anything. My brain was running in all directions looking for answers but each time my head turned to pound and ache. My heart the same. What if she had done something stupid? What if the man had? Only was I to learn later that, in actuality, they hated one and other.

The man never had any patience nor could he understand

the needs of my sister. He would, at times in his frustration, talk to her as if she was worthless, as if she would not understand anything and she hated him for it. She said she would hide, that she tried to ignore him but it didn't help.

He was to return home later that day and although I didn't know of the truth at the time, other than my sister was quite possibly in danger, I couldn't help but build an anger against him, something horribly fierce. He cared not and eventually she called. My sister was never to come home.

**So many times.**

I'm falling — thinking — falling — drinking — falling — blinking — falling — sinking.

**Make the mistakes.**

I have made a mistake.

A mistake, how is that possible?

Mum. She didn't want to be with him any more.

What would make you say that, are you sure?

One day, she had told me she was scared.

Scared of what?

Leaving him.

And how have you made a mistake?

Because I was to keep them together.

I had defended him.

Were you scared?

In honesty, yes. I could only trust him so far.

Did you fear what may have happened had your mother left him?

Yes. I thought the man was capable of anything.

And did you feel responsible to protect your mother?

Of course. What could have I done to protect her?

Why did your mother not leave the man?

Because she was to fall ill.

Did she love him?

Yes, she did love him.

Love does many things which will not make sense to you.

It does not make sense to me.

Love is all the same but everything different.

Please don't do this. This talk. This nonsense.

Can you imagine what has been any way different?

## Hold on.

It was now only the man and I to move again and to a place neither of us wanted to go. The house, narrow, confined, dark and damp, was, by far, the most depressing place to call home. I had already known this was not to last, not for me, as I took the paint to the walls and tried to convince myself once again of better days. I am only here for now but now I am here I must continue to do what I can and if only the man was to think the same, perhaps the future may have been different and better for us both — but no. He could not think like that because depression does not let you! And what am I to do but take it, deal with it and pretend it is all okay?

## Let go.

It was not long after that we ran into another event where we were to be in disagreement again, and the very few good thoughts we had shared between us, almost struggled to exist. Well, the thoughts were weakened to nothing much greater than the tiny threads of a spider's silk web. We were hardly to see each other any more and the few times we did it was too awkward to discuss anything to make the situation we were in any better. We were slowly but surely running out of ground and our narrowing road was destined for nowhere. We were two sorrowful and helpless cases heading for disaster in a distance growing ever closer and neither of us knew if God was to save us or whether we would both end up in hell pleading for life.

**Find out.**

You do realise how strong a spider's silk is, don't you?

**Forget everything.**

I don't understand how the man can treat her like that. How? I am starting to remember many things. Things which I don't want to talk about. Things which actually make me so, so angry it is best to leave this sentence here.

**Start again.**

The time has come
I am guilty
The time has come
We have to move on
The time has come
Let us forget our past
The time has come
They have both now gone

**As love does many things which will not make sense to you.**

There was only darkness in every direction as I walked in through the doors of the house which leaked out a depression from all corners of hollow and emptiness. It was just like an infection — it was to spread over to cover the walls of my colour and leave nothing other than bare ugliness to seep into and onto everything. Everything we had, capturing it like a greed and a fire burning, turning to flame all which it could blame and how the man's mind washed out onto the floors to be swallowed up by the depths of our poverty. We had nothing between us, not any more and how I saw the recession, of him, and his possession of me, clear and how I could only hold dear the thoughts of my mother, of my sister and of my hope, as I had come to tell him my forever and final goodbye. I was scared. I had started to cry from the pain inside as love does many things which will not make sense to you. I didn't want to leave him, I had to leave him to save myself because there was no one else who was going to, other than me. You see, sometimes in life, you have to stand alone to know who you are and who you are not and I have not once forgotten as I go on to find the importance of every single detail, of every single person I have experienced, because I am who they are, and I only, I only hope that the man can stand alone.

**You cannot leave me.**

My heart was torn. Pulled apart and pouring out. I will never forget that day. Walking into the living room, dark and full of smoke, with the television blaring out loud the news of death, the news of hate. The glass of a picture frame smashed all over the floor and with my mother's picture left lying there neglected. Among the dirt and dust, her ornaments of angels broken. A window was kicked in. The man had trashed this place like he had wanted it to be his memories, but memories do not work in such ways.

When I had first walked into the room, I couldn't say anything. He just laid there and ignored me. I then stood there, in the kitchen, looking at all the knives which were left spread across the sides and how sharp they were. I thought of protection but if I was to be hurt, I had honour, unlike my father, to stand up for myself and without cowardice. I had a belief in truth. I had already done all I could. What was to happen was no longer in my hands. I no longer had control. I had gone back into the living room.

'I am sorry but I have to go. I have to leave you.' He was facing the other way when he said back to me, 'Fuck off then.' I told him, again, 'I am sorry. This is not what I want but I have to.' He didn't care. He didn't even react. He just continued to lie there, smoking his cigarette and watching the television. Then, he said, 'You can take your stupid fucking dog.' But when I went to take him the man stopped me, he looked at me then said, 'I am going to go and kill myself and your dog, you dumb, fucked-up cunt.'

## I know.

Manipulation, persuasion, selfishness and hate can lead only to one thing.

## I'll always remember.

And as the people there gathered, I was to see these connections sharing, in life, her and the spirit which was her and the way she had once before softly and unnoticeably passed herself unto them. She was a very popular lady, my mother, with her kind-heartedness and respect for each and every person she had once met, for better and for worse. It was even so that during the funeral, the doors of the church had to remain open as more and more people arrived, including my father, to bless her farewell. I was to think how he must have been feeling since they were to meet at the age of fourteen and had spent most of their days together until the divorce which separated them apart. They were, for a long period of time, most definitely in love and a part of each other and it is not easy, if possible, to let something like that go. Although, he has since then remarried and, so it seemed, moved on. We, the people, rose to see her body carried down the aisle and to where she was going to be rested in peace. Hymns were sung in tradition: Jerusalem was one she had wanted chosen and a friend of ours had covered a recent favourite of hers, Chasing Cars, that she had listened to often when battling the illness, she no longer needed to suffer from. The ceremony, I would imagine like many, was a mixture of both celebration and sadness. It was her wish to be not buried but instead cremated and her ashes to be placed upon the fields we once walked together. I remember once, actually, her telling me it was not leaving this place, her life, that she was afraid of but rather being forgotten in a time to come, a time not too far away. I had said to her to not be so ridiculous, 'As if I, and many others, could forget somebody such as you in years to come, if ever.' And I looked to see a smile. I was to remember that smile when I had to stand in front of the hundreds of faces and express my feelings to everybody there. I had said how she was dear to me and how she would be missed by everyone but I did not particularly enjoy speaking about her, not in this way. For me, I knew it did not matter what I was to say, or how I was to say it; it could never have reflected the truth in the relationship between us.

**I'll always appreciate.**

I know I have said that I had to be strong, to not let my

feelings be seen by those close to me or, in fact, even by those who did not know me so well, but I certainly could not have kept myself together, as much as I had done, without the care and support of a particular family who had, at the time, looked after me as one of their own. They were all great, genuine people who I will never be able to express my real, true appreciation to. God bless.

**In what you and I are able to call home.**

# Chapter Six

## Home?

Home. What is home? Is it a place? Somewhere safe? A feeling? Or a word to heal over wounds of isolation and the promise of peace for the poorer soul?

## I don't know what home is!

Although I am not yet old, I am in such great difficulty to remember a time when I felt as if I belonged: a place to return knowing sweet solitude is available away from all the anxieties of life. In vague memory, I can feel something of a similar kind although I am not entirely sure how much I can speak of this truthfully. It has been several years now since I have joined. The war that is. The war of life. The battle of my brain and heart.

While dear friends have their comforts at home each night with the loves they share in time, I ardently roam the room in which you can call the sky a ceiling where upon light emanates and the walls that surround me are nothing but natures of the earth which keep me in place. I can sleep anywhere. I have done. Yet, I am still enclosed by the concept that man must build himself a home to shelter against the weathers of greater things.

## Do you need to?

I am now sixteen years old and I have lost my father, my

sister, my best friend and I've had to walk away from somebody who has impacted my life so much so I no longer know who I am or what I am to do any more. I've had to leave behind my little dog, many of the people I have met and the place, the village, I had come to love and appreciate in ways I can't express. I guess, a place in which, I would say, had raised me; a place in which, I would say, I was close to calling home. But it wasn't to be. No. I had to go. My journey was to meander down the rivers and roads which wore thinner than a never-ending, forever-darkening memory heading out of happiness. I was starting the path which only a lonely few can walk down.

### For me.

I believe it is one of the worst feelings this world can bring to you: the feeling of being ignored, being forgotten, being left behind. Of not being able to belong, being able to fit in, being able to be a part of everything when we are to know so well, that we are a part of everything but without the opportunity to be ourselves, our true selves. We are nothing but hopeless somethings, hopeless somethings ever trying to escape the skins of our bodies and the dreams of our minds. We are made to feel in all the ways of loneliness without ever really being alone, only alone in the senses of our sincerity, of not being allowed to be who we are actually to be.

### Yes!

I had gone to the place where advice was to be given. Do you know it is quite a difficult thing to, first, admit that you are in need of help and then, second, to do something about it and after that, third, tell a complete stranger your innermost difficulties and personal hardships — especially for somebody still not yet considered an adult? For somebody who is still looking out for something similar to that of a parent. For somebody who is still looking out for a friend they were to once have, before all the chaos swept them away like a hurricane out of season; a storm which had left them alone with a heart darker than the colour black and angrier than a God who thought to create man was a good idea. I had gone to the place where advice was to be given and meetings were to take place once a week.

I had been assigned to a member of staff who, I had been told, was fantastic at his job and a real delight to work with. I had thought to myself how lucky and how fortunate I was for this new chapter to start so well — almost too well. We were to meet once a week at their offices and talk about various thoughts and experiences which I had been finding a struggle to digest and deal with over the past few years. Thoughts and experiences which were not so much receding but more intensifying and advancing into greater thoughts and experiences. However, I was well aware: it was becoming harder for me to tell the difference between the two. Thoughts are one thing. Thoughts can be anything, anywhere, anyone. Experiences are another. Experiences are something in which I have lived.

## Why?

My head hurts. I remember those words. My head hurts. I remember those birds. My head hurts. Should I try again? My head hurts. I love you, amen.

## I am losing it.

76

It is becoming more often than not that I have to miss my days in the classroom so I can work some boring job in order to try and be educated. Basically, I am spending my days numbing my brain knowing I could be where I am supposed to be and working towards a chance of a better life. An educated life. You know, good grades, more friends. To be a part of it.

Hah! I have to laugh. It is all I can do these days. Otherwise I will break. I will fall and keep on falling and I am not the kind of person who can let that happen. I am not the kind of person to give up on myself when I know where I want to be and I know exactly what I want. The thing is, I know I am going to get it. I am and more. That is why I am not the kind to give up.

The worrying part is that I have started talking to myself. The voices in my head are being spoken out and I have no idea where, or who, they are. This place that I am working, instead of actually going to college, is pretty isolated. It is way out in the countryside, somewhere in the fields, on an old farm. I have been cleaning cars. Nice ones. Expensive ones. You know.

But alone, I clean and while it brings me a sense of satisfaction, a sense of tranquillity, a sense of peace away from all the madness, I have voices. These voices are not new but they are, let's put it this way, now steadily growing to be more my friends. It is so that I even listen to what they say. Madness! Yeah, I completely agree! But many times, these voices make sense.

To me they make sense. I have thought, if these voices are just my own thoughts projected in different characters, in different ways, how on earth have I found ways to say things I don't know? I don't get it. Sometimes, it'll take ages to work out what it is that has been said but then it'll suddenly sink in and mostly, to my surprise, I laugh, then appreciate whatever it is.

## Am I going mad?

I have to try, don't I?

You have to try what?

To rebuild a relationship with my father again.

Well, why not?

I haven't forgot the time he had left us.

Do you remember the time when he really tried to leave us?

Yes.

Imagine how he must have been feeling then.

I guess we all go through times when we are to feel hurt.

And, are you to know what may become of such an opportunity?

I really would like to get to know him better.

It may help you with many things which you do not know. So, when and how am I supposed to get in contact with him?

Whenever it is best for you.

What if it goes horribly wrong? What if he doesn't want to know me?

Don't so much avert the past but address it in ways which may help you.

What do you mean by that?

It would be wise to follow up some of these thoughts you are having.

Are you sure?

How will you ever know?

**I am going mad!**

I remember when my father had come over to me at the funeral with tears in his eyes and his arms open wide. I hadn't seen him in years. It was strange to think he was still my father. I remember him telling me that, from now on, he had wanted to be there for us; my sister and I. At this time, I did not know he had built his own house and I did not know so well the woman he had next married. I had liked what he had said to me. I had thought there was some chance things could change. I knew now, things needed to change. We were not to talk to each other after, though I was to keep it in mind that maybe, in the future, we could find some kind of relationship, perhaps friendship, again. I remember when we took a ride on that brand-new, bright red motorbike straight into rays of the sun.

**I need help!**

What to do
I don't know
Haven't a clue
Nothing to show
Who am I
No one to be
All alone
Only me
So here I am
Tell me now
I am talking to you
Show me how

**Don't let me do this!**

79

Nobody had wanted to come with me and, to be honest, it is not like I could blame them. There was this one couple who had offered to drive me close enough to the house. Close enough though far enough away not to be seen and, with that, far enough away to also drive away safe, if to be necessary.

I had gone to break into the house which is now in the name of the man. The man who, when we were last to see each other, had told me he was going to kill himself — and my little dog — on the train track — out behind the back. Two months were to pass by before I knew whether he had or not.

And after those words that he said, I couldn't care less. I mean, I did care, of course I did, but the man had removed himself so far from me there was nothing I could do to help. Not any more. Not now I was to know he did not do what he said he would do and I had realised what he had really done.

The man had only said such words to scare me. Manipulate me. Hurt me. He was never going to go and kill himself. He was just another coward of a man who had come into my life to show me how not to live it, and it is that I must come back to thank him for everything he once taught so well.

**This heaven and hell.**

Nothing is never that far away, nor is everything.

**Wait!**

The house was empty. I mean, it was still full of things that once belonged to my family but empty because the man was not there. I had no idea where he was. It didn't matter. It did. If the man was to come back whilst I was there, I was dead, so at first, I had gotten the police involved to help me.

I had asked the police if they would assist me, help me,

protect me, when I was to go back and take what is mine. And my little dog. And, of course, after much small chitchat of this and that the police were to tell me they could not do anything. They had said I was to need the man's permission!

The house was now in the name of the man and if I was to enter without his permission and take anything with me, it would be seen as burglary. I could, or more so would, be arrested. So, I had said back to the police how ridiculous, how unfair it was and that I will, no matter what, find a way.

One cold dark night in March, I was driven up near to the house. I had taken a bag with me and I was only to wear black clothes. Upon nearing the house, I had looked out for a car on the driveway, there wasn't. I had peered into the front window to see if he was inside, he wasn't. It was time.

### There is nothing you can do!

I hated to look into his eyes and see an innocence, knowing he deserved far more than what has happened and much better than which was going to.

### Forgive me.

I had made contact with my father and, for the first time in the last six, maybe seven, years I think he was to actually realise my life was not going so well, not going so well in the sense that I was no longer to have a life at all. I don't really know what might have been going through his mind before, given the knowledge that he was aware of my mother's illness and he was most certainly au fait with our financial difficulties, considering it was him who had let us struggle down to shackle and stone. Though I am not going to lay hate or blame on him. Not now. I hope never.

All I really want is to find some kind of understanding, some kind of reconciliation with my father over experiences which were, essentially, really neither of our faults to begin with. Perhaps, partly his, if I am to think about how he had treated my mother and why she had decided to divorce him, but I can't go down the avenues which are not so much mine. The question is more, for me, what am I to do with these distances and these differences between us? Is it even so important for me to understand? Is this not, could this be, one way closer to being able to do such a thing?

### I don't need to.
I had to go back and take what is mine.
Yeah, I had to go back to hell.
I mean who would even try and bother?
Yeah, sometimes it is not so easy to be benign.

### If you want change.
So, it was: my problem had not been something I would talk much about with the, let's call him, 'therapist'. It is that I can be very open and honest when I feel like what I have to say wants to be heard however, the meetings we were to have consisted more of practicalities, things such as the possibilities of moving away, the possibilities of financial help with my education and all that similar, etcetera. It was that he, the 'therapist', was to provide some useful information but it was not of help to me as most things these days are based upon the paper and not the person, it was to look as if though my life was not so bad, not really. And I was not to forget my time out in Africa. I knew my life could be far worse than it happened to be but then I was to see everybody else around me, all

looking so happy.

All I wanted was for something to change! With this guy, this 'therapist', I knew nothing was going to change! He was redundant to me, yet he insisted, persisted there was always another possibility, another way, something else and therefore our meetings were to continue on. I was becoming wary of my time with the 'therapist' although there were two things in which I had found beneficial for me. He would buy lunch at our meetings and lunch was something I could not often afford, and the other thing was that I happened to enjoy our routine of meeting up once a week. It was a nice comfort. For the time it lasted anyway. It soon, like everything else, fucked up. He had started texting me at unusual times. He had asked to meet up outside of meetings. He had asked if I had wanted to work at his strip club.

## Look at yourself.

I was to tiptoe around like a hungry cat stalking a lonely mouse and I didn't know which one I was! I didn't want it to be this way, remember?

## Tell yourself the truth!

What was it that you really went back for?

When I had told the man I was going to leave, I didn't have any time to take what was mine. For months, I had to live with only a bag of a few belongings. A few clothes, a couple of photographs but everything was there.

Were you not to be scared that it was possible to see him?

So scared. My heart was beating rapidly into anxiety with the thought he could return at any given minute. I had kept the house lights out and used an old torch that I could turn off far more quickly, if car lights appeared.

Do you think it was really worth the risk?

When I said everything was there, I guess what I had really wanted was to take back all the memories from him. The photographs. The ornaments of now broken angels. My mother's ashes. My mother had also written a diary.

Did you manage to take back all of those things?

No, I didn't have enough time to find everything. The house was in such a mess. I had managed to take a majority of the photographs, the now broken angels, my mother's ashes, passports, certificates, clothes, but not her diary.

Do you think the man still has it?

I wouldn't know whether he would've kept it safe or if he would've instead burnt it in anger. Only the man knows which. It was the diary my mother had written during her final year. It was the diary I had never got to read.

Do you think you'll ever go back?

I don't think I could, it would be too dangerous. First, I had broken in through the back door and it was possible I could be found guilty. Second, and more likely, if the man was to see me he would most probably kill me.

## I can't.

What on earth and in God's name is that beautiful monstrosity, seriously? My father had asked if I had wanted to move in with him. He said there was plenty of space in the new house he was now living in. He said that I would be welcome to begin a new life, a new life there, and to start again.

At first, I had genuinely thought it to be a good idea. I had really thought this was going to be the change that I had wanted. I had really thought this was going to be the change that I had needed. Unfortunately, it was not so. All was to restore thereafter when I was to see, when I was to realise.

This new house, this new house of his was not just some house. It was the building which stood before my life's demolition. It was the foundation to which buried underneath my burning pain. My father had once forgotten me, not cared for me, but had managed to build himself a fucking home?

## I am dead.

I had almost forgotten the Pyramids of Giza. We had gone to Egypt on a family vacation. Only young and a long time ago now. How strange it was to see a prison. How strange it was to see a religion. Next to each other down at the bottom. How my father and I descended so far. It feels similar to something I've seen before. And in before I am to mean now. In this house, I want wasted and rotten. This house I want burnt to the ground.

## Under all the layers.

She was devious, malicious, offensive, provocative, harmful and bitter. She was also smart, sharp, determined, inventive, careful and favourable.

## — Cold.

The wicked witch had been married to my father for a few years now. They were the ones who had built the house together — the oh so happy home, in which I happened to fall haplessly into. My stepmother, I should say, was not so bad really though evil can present itself as good, can it not?

## — Careless.

I mean I swear she was a wicked witch. My stepmother.

Honestly. She hated me. It sounds as though I am being horrible, but she was horrible. Maybe, possibly. She was really nice to others. Maybe others deserved her being really nice to them. I don't know but I do know that she actually hated me.

## — Censored.

She just laughed at me. She laughed at me because I had written with the condensation on my bathroom window, 'one day I will be famous'. Nobody was supposed to see it. It was only for me. I did it to keep myself motivated. There were times, often, when I had actually wanted to give everything up.

## — Chained.

I cannot say sorry. She, my stepmother, had belittled me in ways just like the man had done so before, and there is no way now I will allow myself to take this from them any more! No way. For the entirety of the time I was to live with them, I could not honestly tell who became worse between the two.

## I can't take this any more!

This other time, I was coming down the spiral staircase when, at the bottom, she was sitting opposite to where I was standing: she was working from home and my father was working away. She turned to look at me to make some sorry remark. Well, sorry is the wrong word. She wasn't sorry in the slightest. There, as the laptop lighted her evil-looking face and all I had wanted was to leave the house as quickly as I could, she, my stepmother, stopped me to tell me how everything, everything, was my fault.

My fault! They were her actual words! She had said to me that I was naïve. That I was a dreamer to believe life was going to get better if I was to carry on the way I was to be. That it was not hope, not love, that I had needed but instead solitude and discipline away from my past. She said, I had to move on. I just had to leave it all behind. Forget it. Forget everything. My mother. The man. She neither cared much for my sister. They, her and my father, didn't even help my sister when she wasn't to have a place to live!

That's right. A year or so before I came to stay at the house, my sister — remember when she ran away from me? — had asked them if it was possible to live with them. And their response, of course I wasn't to know this until after, otherwise these words would be very much different, was no. They had said no! Their reason being, it would be too much for them. It would bear too heavily on their relationship. To take care of my sister would be too much for them! My sister was homeless and they did not care.

I mean can you really believe I am telling the truth because sometimes I can't, even though I am. And the other thing she had told me, my wicked witch of a stepmother, was the reason why I didn't have a relationship with my father. She had said to me, all I was ever interested in, from him, was his money. Can you imagine at the ages of eight, nine, ten, eleven and through to my mother's death at the age of fifteen, I was to think money is all I had wanted from him? I had wanted a father who was to care for us.

### Take me away from here!
Stretched back neck.
Swollen gut.
My mind.
Blunt cut.

Pressured veins.
Poisoned liver.
A crooked twist in the body of night.
The devil's master makes me shiver.
Drowned out hope.
No turning back.
Left outside cold.
The only colour, black.
The voices speak aloud.
Much harm is to be said.
It is right that I must finish the bottle.
Now that I live wishing I was dead.

## I'm desperate.

I was hardly to be there — I mean it was to be almost warlike between us. There was this one time I had managed to stay in a different bed for eleven nights in a row. Well, I don't think I was really to blame for it. They didn't want me around. That is how they were to act towards me most of the time.

## I'm done.

Why do you feel it is necessary to drink so much?

Most of the time, it is the only way in which I can escape far enough.

Escape far enough from what exactly?

From life, what else do you think?

Yourself.

Well, look at everything which has happened to me.

I am.

Do you think this is what I want? Who I want to be?

Yes.

Are you doing this on purpose?

Are you making everything worse?

Can you not see that I am trying?

I can see that you are starting to believe that you are somebody you are not.

What?

You are already starting to forget who you are and why you are to be here.

Then tell me who I am?

I am.

Honestly.

Because I really don't care any more.

Yes, you do.

How do you even know me?

Believe me, I know you.

Just go. Seriously. Just go.

I'll be around when you are to want me again.

Do you hear me? Just go.

## Give me the chance to run.

It wasn't a very good car to begin with, to be honest, but it was the freedom that I had needed in order to get away from my father, when living with him in his big house of small dreams, at least for me, because what I had in mind to find, he had run away from a long time ago. And it needed addressing that he was regressing and I was advancing into a state of manic mania — I had wanted it to be true — I had wanted to live my life as if it was to be a film or a dream and so it was to sometimes seem, from the things which were to keep on happening to me, it was quite the chaos I had hoped for at the age of sixteen to seventeen. Life was to continue on, mean, and

I had come to realise a couple of years ago, that I had next to nothing to lose, because I can't, it is not possible — nothing is ever mine and nothing is ever yours. Unless you and I are to submit to one thing and one thing only, but when the idea sits so lonely, it comes across so phoney and who are you and I to believe in such nonsense, such rubbish. Let's forget it, let's get back into the car and drive on home. And, when I say home I mean let's just drive. So we did just that until we were to come underneath a bridge and hit ice, black ice, which laid unnoticed out of town, it was to throw me down, it was to chuck my car across the road and smash straight into the post before flipping over onto its side and far into the darkness — fuck this.

## I want to let go.

I am not going to blame them. No. I can't do that. I can't blame them for what they had done. No. I am not going to blame them. It was fair for them to do it. No. I definitely can't say that. It was probably, in the end, the best thing that could have happened. Yes. Absolutely. I can definitely say that!

It was by letter. They had sent a letter to some friends of mine and it was to read of my eviction from their house, the house. As I was to read it aloud, I was to laugh. I mean, it was really of no surprise to me. Not at this point. My friends, an older couple, were to cry but for me laughter was far better.

It was the day after my birthday. I hadn't invited them to the celebration because I had wanted to celebrate. They were not to know, from me, of any celebration so whether they did know about it or not, I don't know, but if they were to, then, did you really think I would have wanted you there?

Of course, I had wanted you there! I had wanted you there all of my life but where were you to be? Where have you been?

Where are you now? I have no idea of who you are or what you are to think of me, whether you care or if you are still even alive? I've had to etch you out like a mistake!

I do not believe it would have been the deciding factor of my eviction — the not inviting them to my celebration part. But I am aware it would have been quite hurtful, especially to my father. I had invited everyone else and there must have been over a hundred and something people to show for it.

But what was I to do, pretend everything was to be okay? I was done with pretending. I didn't even care that I was now homeless, officially homeless. All I had wanted was change. All I had wanted was for somebody to care. To care truthfully and not pretend in the faces of fear and forget who I am.

At least now I have come to understand why those many people at the bar wanted to drink so much. In one way or another, no matter how big or how small their situations were to be, I could see that everybody wanted out — they had wanted to let it out but they feared they would lose too much.

Us people want to wrap ourselves up in chaos and carry on through the mayhem with the hope that one day it will all become blue skies and big smiles, and why can we not believe in that? What is wrong believing in that? Is it not within hope and faith to which makes us feel most alive?

**Please, just let me be who I am!**

I had once heard 'loneliness is a gift'. I think it is. But then so is insanity.

Thanks Bukowski. No, seriously. I mean, it is. We are just people, are we not?

# Chapter Seven

**Him.**

Don't be afraid, she told me.

**Her.**

If you had one more chance, would you think to change your life? Would you think to consider yourself as somebody who is happy?

What would you do if somebody was to take everything away tomorrow? Would you live today in all the same ways or think to change your life?

**Him.**

I have lost
My inspiration
I have lost
My loving touch
I have lost
My imagination
I have never wanted much

**Her.**

It is much easier to be alone than to be surrounded by the wrong people.

**Him.**

Love is madness.

**Her.**

Not being allowed, or not feeling comfortable, to be yourself is madness.

**Him.**

Don't abuse what is a gift.

**Her.**

It is far better and greater understood through the opposite of what it is.

**Him.**

I don't know
Who I am
I don't know
Where to go
This world spins so fast
Around me
Faster than I can grow

**Her.**

I am scared of what I can do, so I tell myself I can't.

**Him.**

I look at myself in the eye and see nothing.

**Her.**

You can fear anything in this life, especially love.

**Him.**

Everything has time to experience itself, again and again.

**Her.**

Did she ever know just how beautiful her smile was?

**Him.**

I have tried
To understand
I have tried
To work things out
Everything is an experience
For that
I have no doubt

**Her.**

Dance to the beat of the drum which is life.

**Him.**

Nothing is going to cost more than time spent in negativity.

**Her.**

Other people will not always be who you would like them to be.

**Him.**

In our greatest times of difficulty, our biggest misunderstanding is love.

**Her.**

Be entirely grateful: for if there is to be nothing, you are also nothing.

**Him.**

Tell me
What does it mean?
I guess
We'll never know
This loneliness inside
Is killing me
Very slow

**Her.**

If I am not learning, I am not living.

**Him.**

'Let it be' was often mentioned but those who did not hear never listened.

**Her.**

You cannot change what is, you can only change what is not.

**Him.**

I am quite sure all the best people are mad.

**Her.**

I will test you, I will put you through hell but I will love you.

**Him.**

I want
To be set free
I have tried
My best to stay
To a place
Where I can be me
There is no other way

**Her.**

All is real, but a dream it is.

**Him.**

May we forget for a while but not forever.

**Her.**

So much love is lost in fear.

**Him.**

The irony is that we're trying to teach lessons we're yet to learn ourselves.

**Her.**

Not one thing can be perfect, only everything.

**Him.**

I tell myself
I am not scared
For who
Am I to blame?
I had only wanted happiness

But my feelings
Stay the same

**Her.**

We may run but we do know there is nowhere else that we can go.

**Him.**

She was the best thing that had ever happened to me
Her hair, her eyes, her smile, her love, I cannot explain
She danced just like the spirit I have tried so hard to be
Her secret and everything she was, had taken away my pain

**Her.**

Time for time, if you cannot give me yours then I cannot give you mine.

**Him.**

I guess it is starting to get to me
This thing that is not meant to be
This hidden life, my other entity
Where did I go, why cannot you see?
Believe me, this is not my fantasy
To live in a mind of complete slavery
To run around town so helplessly
Desperately explaining my own mentality
And when no one takes me seriously
Carelessly doing acts of complete stupidity
My hopeless attempts to set myself free
I guess it is starting to get to me

**Her.**

He who is to discover God is he who is to discover himself.

**Him.**

Give me a place to sleep. Anywhere, I don't care.

Give me a pillow and a blanket. It's the coldness I can't bear.

Give me some food and water. My stomach hurts, my mouth is dry.

Give me some of your attention. Come over and look me in the eye.

**Her.**

He likes to think I do not know.

**Him.**

I am
So tired.
Fired from
Freedom, itself
Has decided
To go.
Left with
Little to Decide,
It's time
To reside
With these
Thoughts of
Fire, blistering

My mind.
I am
So tired.

**Her.**

You really do have to love yourself before you can love
anybody else.

**Him.**

The cold and lonely bitterness
Brings realisation to my life in this world
This journey I am on is now lost in all my thoughts
There is nowhere I want to go at this time

**Her.**

Stand strong. Have faith. Be patient.

**Him.**

I'm down. I'm out.
I scream. I shout.
I'm angry. I'm scared.
Who listens? Who cares?
Not you. Not me.
No more. It cannot be.
This life. Give it up.
It hurts. It sucks!

**Her.**

I know how strong I am because I know how weak I can
be.

**Him.**

Don't be afraid, she told me.
Don't be afraid, she told me.
Don't be afraid, she told me.
Don't be afraid, she told me.

**Her.**

I love you.

**Him.**

If this is a cry for help, then I do not want your sympathy

I do not want your sad faces nor a false attempt of empathy

If you try to understand then try your best to stand with me

I know it is not easy but all I want to experience is humanity

**Her.**

I am here for you.

**Him.**

How does she do it?

**Her.**

We are all here just trying to find our way back home.

# Chapter Eight

**Be myself?**

All I am trying to do is get to where I want to be; it is the hardest thing anyone has to do in their life.

**Bless you.**

God, I want you as a close friend. I do because I don't have many any more but at this point in my life I have to hold onto the little sanity I have left.

**Are you being serious?**

I had nothing when they were to call me up, when they were to tell me I could go and stay with them for a while until I was able to get my life back together, at least try to get my life back together again. I had nothing. This couple, they were good friends of my mother back when, had offered to me a room in their house, their new house in the village where I was once very close to calling home. The place I had never wanted to leave, but had to. The place that was to keep hold onto many of my memories: the man, if he was still around, and more importantly, my sister, if she was.

**Bemusing?**

It was so hard not to; it was so nice there. To think of it as 'home', I mean.

## What?

It was the first time in years where I had a place to come back to, to relax and let go of whatever or whoever may have made my life more difficult than it needed to be that day. It was the first time in years where I had a place to come back to, to put down the weight I carried with me everywhere and so heavy, so heavy I had to question repeatedly if it was still necessary.

But it wasn't a choice back then, even if it was. It was just nice to know I had a place to return to. The couple I was staying with were so incredibly kind. They were the kind of people not everybody in life gets the chance to meet, and even if so, not the chance to get to know properly at least. I would like to think I am very much one of the lucky ones. Often, I would.

The couple were to take really good care of me; they were to actually care for me and genuinely. They would ask each night if I would like to sit down with them, to be in their company whether it was to watch the television or to talk about a subject of interest we shared or even, at times, to go out into the village and have a drink. They wanted me to be around.

A number of occasions, we would have dinner at the dining table which was great but somewhat rather strange; it seemed so sophisticated! The food, the wine, the guests and the conversations were all things I was not used to, although had wanted. It was to remind me very much of my first years — the atmosphere, the cosiness, the warmth, the togetherness. It was nostalgic.

## You have all broken me!

It is as the flame burns my mind flickers

In and out of consciousness, fragile like the heart
The heart that's been broken, one too many times
Is there any way I can trust it again?

## Do you not get it?

Where is he? What is he doing? Is he okay? Does he still think of me? Does he know that I still think of him? That I miss him. That he, besides how I can express it at times, has impacted my life in ways I cannot be more thankful for. He has changed my life. The man. I remember being so scared of everything when I was younger. So scared. I was frightened to do anything. I was frightened to do anything I didn't know. I was frightened to do anything on my own. He has changed my life. He was the one to give me my name. He had given me the confidence to go out and try new things. The confidence to go out and meet new people. The confidence to go out into the darkness and to be able to stand alone. We used to go and watch the football together. Spend so much time together. Share many of the same experiences together. He had looked after me. I had wanted to look after him. I promise, I didn't want to leave you. I had to. He has changed my life.

## Of course not.

They don't see it
They won't see it
Tears that I cry
Tears that I hide

## I need her.

God, I miss her. I miss her so much. What can I do? It has been so long now. My sister. My sister! I have let her down. I don't know what I can do. I don't! It hurts me just to think of her. To think she had to run away from me. To think she could not even tell me how she was feeling. How was she feeling? I can't let myself even think of this... I had let her down when she had needed me most; when I had promised our mother I would take care of her. I have failed. I have failed! It makes me feel sick. I want to be sick. Please, help me... Please, help her! All I have ever wanted was to be able to give her what she deserves and she deserves more than this... this life we share.

**You are so afraid.**

Have you ever put yourself in a position where death is staring straight at you — calling you — wanting you — tempting you — begging you — believing in you? Do it. Come on. Do it. Do it! Don't be scared. Don't look down...

No! Fuck off. Don't do this to me. Again! Fuck. Go. Get out of my head. Go. Fuck.

**Is it so obvious?**

My stepmother once said something to me I had to learn and understand. Her words, the words, were: 'the world owes you nothing'. I had hated her for it but she was right. The world really does not owe me anything. And why would the world owe me? Why would the world owe anybody? Why would we, why would I, assume that you and I are better than, more important than, the world itself? That the world is indebted to us, to me!

What then are we, am I, to do if the world was to never pay up? If we, if I, were to never receive the fortune we, I, believe we deserve — we, I, deserve for being here and in person! Do we, do I, then need to start reacting in ways for ourselves, myself, to cope with this great confusion? The needing of our, my, purpose, the needing of our, my, reason and our, my, needing to be needed. Why do we, I, suffer so often in this place so unknown to us, to me?

## Beyond a shadow of a doubt.

I have now finished my education and I have now turned eighteen, the age in which one is legally considered an adult in many countries worldwide.

What am I to do now I am considered an adult? Am I now supposed to be responsible for myself and the decisions that I make? How can I be though?

I have no idea what to do; I am nowhere near close to knowing what to do. I fear at every turn, thinking I will go the wrong way and with that, alone.

## Remember me.

This is not what I want to be doing but I do understand this is what I must be doing if I am to get anywhere close to where I would, one day, like to be.

You see, some of us do not get the opportunity to work a job that we can say is more than just earning money, and just enough money to keep on living.

And it is so unforgiving to not live life passionately and at the best of your ability. To wake up another day unhappily is not what you or I should do.

## Do you see?

I have got to do it, I have got to go back there. I can still hear it, I can still feel it: Africa, Africa! The place I was once to be alive, the place I was once to belong. At least in a way more than the UK, the United Kingdom that to me I do not feel so united with. Not any more. And not because I do not want to be either; more because I am not allowed to be is a statement much closer. Those who are not the same do not fit in, they do not adhere to the rules and regulations of the society and this is something that just cannot be. To put it most simply, one has the choice to change, or to be changed, before bordering a point completely unaccepted by the ways of 'normality'.

**By her side with her head held high and her handbag and her hat.**

I will tell you this in the exact ways I can remember it happening, yet please don't, not for one moment, think I am trying to convince you of something that not even I am capable of believing in myself. It is just a memory, it is only another story, or that of another experience I have been given and further presented through my own interpretation. It really does not mean too much; however, I do think it is something worth mentioning.

The encounter occurred once after I had closed the bar, joined my friends back at the house where an after party was taking place, and much later on in the night when everybody had already made their ways back home. I was not to realise, straight away, that I had remained alone, as I talked to this girl in which the house belonged... we were caught up laughing and joking until about four or so o'clock early on in the cold winter's morning.

It was then I was to leave her and walk off into the darkness behind where we were standing, exiting the small, circle-shaped cul-de-sac and onto an extremely narrow road which ran up and adjacent to the main street leading past the church and the traffic lights. The road, that I had no choice but to walk down, was only of use to the residents of the very few houses, and so it was to be very much private and really not very well lit.

The distance I had to walk down the darkened road was close enough to fifty metres, and to my left side ran a stream of water making me shiver even colder than I was already to be that night. It was to my right there stood one more house, fifteen metres away, with a wooden gate crossing over the entrance of the driveway and a densely thick hedgerow bordering the property from one end to the other and creating a sense of claustrophobia.

It is that I have learned to walk, wherever I am, with my head up and my back straight so it is to look as if, even if I do not, I know where I am going. It is also that, in the village this experience had taken place and it is the place I had gone back to once having left before, everybody knows, or at least acknowledges, each other in meeting. So, of course, only as I was to walk along on my own, I had happened to see an elderly lady ahead of me.

Upon seeing her my first thoughts were to speak aloud and say hello, thinking it would make her feel a little less anxious about another person walking around at this hour in the morning. But then my second thoughts prevented me doing so as I was to think she could, perhaps, become rather frightened and consider me a drunk or some other form of trouble and feel far and much more uncomfortable. With this in mind, I had stayed silent.

I was keeping a close eye to my right and over towards her but looking as though I was not doing so, just in case. The elderly lady first opened up the gate before entering out forward onto the dark, narrowing road in which I was walking down. She was somewhat of a smallish lady, petite in figure although strong in posture and she carried with her a handbag which fell over her left shoulder. I could also see her wearing some kind of old hat.

She was to come across to me as confident and it was then I had started to wonder what on earth is she doing, and where could she possibly be going, so early in the morning? No shops were to be open for at least another two to three hours and she was not to have a dog to take out or a car to drive to a place where life may be more awake at this time. Questions continued to race my mind as it was now me who was starting to feel a little panicked.

Thoughts then emerged if she was okay. It may be that she has become senile, that she has unfortunately lost her knowledge of time, of space and now roams at her fancy without any awareness of her environment and her exposure. It could be a danger for her to be doing such a thing and, if it was to be a danger, was it something for me to be concerned of, that I should be dealing with considering the fair uneasiness of the situation?

Not sure, I had continued to carry on, with the distance between us closing, and the wanting to stop was, at this point, impossible. It would have suggested something strange as we were now virtually walking side by side. Then, I had frozen completely. I honestly could not believe in what I was to be seeing. The elderly lady's face was perfectly transparent and so was her body as she continued to walk with me with her arms gently swinging.

**God?**

I hate it.

Hate what?

Why this is all about me and not about her?

What is all about you and not about her?

This story.

This story is about her just as much as it is about you.

That is not true, she has been through so much and it is not mentioned.

Can you write down her story?

No, but I wish I could.

How well could you write down her story?

Not very well, not very well at all.

Why is that?

Please don't.

Please don't what?

You know that I don't know my sister, how could I write down her story?

How does this make you feel?

Honestly?

Of course, you do not have to say anything.

It is not that I don't want to, it is just that I don't know how to.

Try to.

I try not to think about it, if I am to be truthful.

Think about the relationship between you and your sister?

I don't even know what our relationship is.

Do you love her?

Of course, I love her.

Do you show her?

No, well, not really.

Do you want to?

Yes, why would I not?

Then why is it that you do not?

Because I cannot!

What is stopping you?

That is the question, I don't know how to!

Do you love others and show them?

Yes, but it is not the same.

Why is it not the same?

Because they have not experienced what my sister has.

How does that make a difference in showing your love?

Because I do not have to feel guilty about it.

So, you are to feel guilty about loving your sister?

I owe my sister something more than whatever love is.

## Pass over to me that bottle.

It is the worst thing out there for me, but I cannot help going back to it, keep on going back to it, keep on drinking it and continue letting it poison my mind, my body. It is like somebody is wanting to kill me. Somebody inside is wanting to kill me but it is not me. It is somebody like me, but hiding under another identity, waiting for me to drink and finish the bottle they first handed to me. When I was too young and weak to see what harm it would eventually do to me, when I was too young to know any better than those who were older and surrounded me. When I had looked up to those people and thought this is how life is supposed to be and are they all not getting along so happily? Of course I am speaking of this rhetorically, because I am to look back now and think actually just how ridiculous, just how pathetic, and just how dumb we, no, just how dumb I am, because it is me who cannot help going back to it, keep on going back to it, keep on drinking it and continue letting it poison my mind, my body. It is like somebody is wanting to kill me. Somebody inside is wanting to kill me and, it is only me. I am the one who is hiding under another identity, waiting for me to drink and finish the bottle I first handed to me. The nights I choose to drink alone trying to avoid any reflections I don't want to see, the nights I choose to drink alone because I don't want to face the truth, the reality. The nights when I accidently look at myself in the mirror and think this is how life is going to be, and am I not getting along so happily? Of course, I am speaking of this rhetorically, because I am to look forward now, and think actually just how ridiculous, just how pathetic and just how dumb we, no, just how dumb I am, because it is me who cannot help going back to it, keep on going back to it, keep on drinking it and continue letting it poison my mind, my body…

## Who am I?

He would have got it if he had wanted it, I would have stopped at nothing to protect my sister that day. And it worries me that there are times when I am ready to exert all of my pain onto another. Of course, I should say, it would have to be something serious enough for me to do so, but then again, anybody who would even attempt to hurt somebody close to me is enough.

More than enough, because I am done with people taking advantage of others in this life, in my life — to those who are to surround me, to those I am to love and to care about. And I am not the type to scream and shout out the wants for a fight just to express the size of my… ego, I am not like that, but it would not phase me too much to lose myself to a place in prison.

## Is not that quite the question to ask?

Have you ever heard of the expression 'the light at the end

of the road'? They are great words of hope, aren't they? They are great words to make you feel a lot better when nothing else ever goes right for you, aren't they?

It was the third of January and a beautiful day in the heart of the city when my friend and I embarked on a journey of forty miles all along the grand banks of the River Thames to Big Ben and the Houses of Parliament.

We were heading out on this adventure to fundraise as much money as we could (one thousand five hundred pounds!) for a wildlife conservation project I was soon to be volunteering on out in the Limpopo, South Africa.

Instead of going straight to university, to my surprise I did get the grades despite the fact my attendance often averaged below thirty percent each week, I had wanted to do something I knew impacted my life once before.

I had wanted to give and I had wanted to give to myself a new experience in a new place and obviously, I thought, where better than Africa? I was still remembering Uganda and if I was to take anything from what I had learnt so far.

The journey was to begin on the south-west side of the city and actually as far down as Woking, a district in the county of Surrey. There, where we were to start at sunrise, is a tributary of the Thames named the River Wey.

As we were to make our way along the tributary, with appreciation to the very early start, the sun was to greet us through the bare branches of the lightly frosted trees which brought about a happiness to our conversation.

'Look at the ways of the foliage!' my friend had said to me as I was to cry out with laughter! He was so right, the scenery was something spectacular, something amazing, yet we, two teenage boys, were talking so fondly of nature?

We were to continue our path onward where soon enough the Thames was to rush by our feet and bring about an enormous sense of energy, of prosperity, and to add the picturesque properties sitting on the banks too.

It was quite the journey we were on and only by foot! Forty miles is more or less a marathon and a half and, if the truth is to be told, we did little to no preparation for it; our only preparation was to believe we would do it!

The hours progressed and the sun kept shining for the people who were out with us to catch the warmth of the winter. Our route was to pass many popular places such as Hampton Court, Kew Gardens and Battersea Park.

These areas: absolutely stunning. It was also very pleasing to see the people appreciating, sharing even, the beauty of nature which surrounded them. However, it was also the architecture making the environment memorable.

When I walk, I like to both wander and wonder through the places my feet lead me and imagine in all the ways that I can find possible, in all the shoes that have been before, the shoes that are, and the shoes which will.

It is certainly a city of courage, isn't it? As it stands so strong with its power and might to influence, to influence its country, and to be home to such royalty. And a city so diverse with worldwide knowledge and great history.

Sometimes I like to think of it as a mystery: why here, why now and, what does it mean to me? I was actually born somewhere near to where we have passed today. Not for me to call it home, of course, we moved from there on.

'Wow, now I am drifting' is what I have got to be thinking, though there is much which can be said about this journey. But as darkness draws an end to daylight and my friend and I see the light, the bright lights of the city...

I look towards a lamp-post, one hundred metres ahead of me and, about one hundred metres in front of Westminster Bridge, the last bridge to cross over, and strangely, the only lamp-post not to be brightening the streets beneath.

In my head so tired, thoughts caught my attention, thoughts of my mother, and I had started to hear myself speak, 'Would she be proud of me today? Would she be proud of me these past three years? Am I doing it, life, right?'

'What if I am not? What if I am running around hopelessly trying escape life all too easily? What if I am seeking sympathy with the same level of enthusiasm as a musical director of an orchestra performing a symphony?'

Then I had said, 'Mother, God, if you are still with me please can you show me a sign? For when I eventually get to the lamppost, in one hundred metres time, can you do this thing for me and make what is broken, shine?'

# Chapter Nine

**What is the point?**

There are certainly some things in life that look beautiful, seem beautiful and are called beautiful before they are to one day, suddenly, disappear.

Disappear into the places which are soon to become forgotten, soon to become inconsequential, insignificant, unimportant and unnecessary.

And do they disappear because they are not what we really once thought? I had to question myself, what did it mean to me; how did I feel about it?

**All joking aside.**

To think, to feel, to hurt, be real
To live, to love, to fall, under above
To run, to hide, to laugh, don't abide
To seek, to be, to know, you're me

**It is nothing more than nothing.**

The two raced across the frosted fields with their arms open wide like how the birds use their wings to glide through the many different skies high up

above and there, as their mother looked on, the trees stood like naked silhouettes in front of a misted backdrop haze, mirroring the black and white keys of a beautiful piano, a piano which touched upon the end of her fingertips and the end of his thoughts as the father started to wander

over the fields that are left empty, there are no children and there is no mother to play on a cold winter's day and for a heart in need of warmth.

## How do you know?

In order to live
You must let go
Of fear
And to let go
Of fear
You have to believe

## Get experience.

And that is what I had done, flown to South Africa on my own without knowing who I was going to spend the next several months with and out in the wild, out in the Limpopo where nature surrounds you all but forever.

It is where nature takes your heart and reluctantly gives it back to you unless you are to want it, I mean really want it in the sense that you are to want life. And then to realise you are a part of it, almost only an insignificant part of it!

If I am to be honest, the real reason why I had decided to do it was because I had to get away from everything. I had to get away from what I was to consider normal yet was not normal and go to a place where death is life.

A place where I had wanted to put a death to my past and start over with a new light and a new hope, a hope to find a new way to be me. It is that I had wanted to see how the lion is able to rule the wild and respect it the same.

## What?

I am not able to explain it — I can't! All the experiences, all the animals, the people, the friends, the friends that I had made, the things that I had done, the things I was to learn about myself... I can't explain any of that!

## Is it not obvious?

I was back to cleaning cars when this van pulled up beside me and a guy shouted out my name, his face looked familiar, I had recognised him, but I did not know him — at least not very well, anyway. The guy was a local carpenter from our village. He seemed to be successful in his work and likeable in his personality, which was what I had perceived from the conversation we were to have. He needed an assistant to help him over the busier months of the summer and, with the consideration I was not to overly enjoy cleaning cars and I had a few months spare, I was to say yes.

## No! Is a house on fire not a bad thing?

The guy and I got on like a house on fire — I have never got that expression!

## Is it your choice?

Why is it that somebody can come into your life, somebody you have been waiting for all of your life, then after a few moments they are gone again?

## Everything has its time.

The hyena's jaw bites down hard — crunching everything, even bone — into its scavenging gut. Craving flesh, blood and anything it desires, it attacks with a hackle and a scream as the females hunt, together being clever though evil too. The look of hunger. The look of discomfort, their bodies declivous to tail, their faces fake smile as mouths open up to teeth which look sharper than obsidian glass, and how they can slash into the sinews of the innocent running prey. But I was not running, I was just sleeping! Out there on the riverbed, catching some forty winks under the stars after midnight, after my duty — two hours each we looked after one another in the middle of the bush. Though there was no sign of trouble, not that I was to know anyway before the morning when friends then told me they had to scare off hyenas only ten foot away from me. They were staring straight at me, licking their lips all juicy virtually tasting me already…

## This is true.

The guy was good to me. He helped me a lot when he really didn't have to. He was kind, kind-hearted and strong, head-strong. But he was different. The guy was surely not stereotypical of the image others may have thought. He was to believe in life and made choices to live the way he had wanted.

## Christ!

The wild had wakened me; no longer could I tolerate society. Back home is not what it used to be; this place pulls me down like an unwanted gravity.

## I need another drink.

We were to drink an awful amount of alcohol together. Looking back, it was most probably how we got to know one another so well, actually. Most nights, we could easily go through a bottle of vodka, or gin, or the occasional brandy, but that was more his taste than mine. You see, he was far older than me. In fact, he was old enough to be my father, yet I was to consider him to be more of a brother, to be honest. I would say a brother, something more than just a good friend with a good heart. I had liked the way he was to care about me, look out for me and want the best for me. He was always the most positive. Positively confident and, without a doubt, an enjoyable person to work with and to socialise with. Alongside this, he was also a great entertainer and generously fair when it was time to deal with anything financial — he had even, once or twice, helped me by lending to me and I do wonder, without his help, what I would have done otherwise. Like my father, the guy was to have money, quite a lot of money and he had earnt it, being highly skilled in his profession and well-known for it. It was another thing I was to admire in his character, I guess. I knew I was going to learn a lot and, with that, I was to hope, have a great friendship.

### Perhaps it was only a dream?

They had said this kind of thing does not happen, not like this. Not all of them and definitely not the entire herd of twenty-three elephants along with their young so cute and clumsy. They had us completely surrounded! Trumping their trunks and waving their big African ears, blowing up dust and making a scene so beautiful. It really could have been all so different!

### Perhaps.

There was a time when I had thought to join the army and this was only because I was ready to give up on everything, all that I had once believed before had gone and, more, I was ready to surrender and give my life away.

**Please tell me how.**

I had received a phone call literally not a few days after starting work with the guy, the carpenter, and although I was not to recognise the number, I was to recognise the voice, it was a voice I hadn't heard in years.

Probably, at least, five years. It was a girl I was somewhat fond of when we were younger and she would travel down south to visit her father who happened to live just opposite to me. She was a really sweet girl actually.

The contact we had was to come to an end as our lives developed. We were both to become far busier, our lives were to become more complicated, and with such a distance apart our little likeness for each other drifted with it.

It was nothing serious, of course, but a shame that our friendship had reached its conclusion so soon into what could have been its beginning. Though life has its ways, I have come to learn. There is a reason, no doubt.

About it, the phone call... I had absolutely no idea why she was calling me and how she was to even get a hold of my number in the first place. Yet, before I could even respond a hello, she was to hurriedly speak in panic.

She said, 'Your little dog, I have him here with me at the vets. I need your help.' I was so confused, how could she possibly have my little dog, which not even I had seen in over three years, and to be half way up the country?

And to be at the vets! 'What?' I had said back to her.

'Your dog, your little dog that we once used to walk together, is here. I have him here at the vets and he is going to be put down to sleep if I am not able to pay the charges.'

She continued, 'They have told me it is going to cost around a thousand pounds for the operations, for the medicines, and all I can do is ask you. Are able to do it? Or, unfortunately, I am so sorry, I really can't afford it.'

She was in tears. I felt awful. I was still not even to know how this had all happened. And worse, I did not have a thousand pounds, I did not have a hundred pounds. My heart dropped as I realised this was my only chance.

It was my first and only chance I could do something to save my little dog. For everything which has happened with the man, the way it had ended, I have felt nothing but guilt for my mistake not to have taken him with me.

My little dog, that is. Why did I think to put others before my little dog who was innocent in all of what had been, in all that he had seen and to such violence which made him shake and shiver all lonely in the corner?

'Give me one minute,' I replied in false confidence. I had run inside to the guy who I have said was like a brother to me. I was to very quickly explain the situation and asked if it was in any way possible to borrow the money.

As we were planning to work over the last of the summer together he, which I cannot thank him enough — I hope he is to know, advanced me a sum to cover the cost of the veterinary charges and, more so, offered support.

I really do have so much respect for him, in his bold kindness and good spirit. Without a moment to spare, I picked up the phone and called back. 'Yes, go ahead with it… I can pay!' I couldn't think about it any other way.

No, I cannot imagine it. No. No. My friend, the girl, had said she needed to sort out all things her end before getting back to me with the explanation of events and I can remember just sitting there silent, completely perplexed.

It wasn't too long before she was to call back, thank goodness. She seemed to be much calmer and, God bless her, had opened up with an apology for getting in touch with me out of the blue, but I had said she should not be.

'You are sorry? For what you have just done? Don't be silly. You have just saved my little dog! Do you have any idea of what that means to me?' Then I was to ask her how this all happened, how was my little dog to be there?

'The man. The man had come to stay at our house for a while because he knew my mum. They have been friends ever since school though I didn't know about it. When my parents divorced, my mum decided to move here.

The man said that he did not have anywhere to live for a while so my mum took him in, she was only trying to be kind to him. Then, after a couple of weeks, and his behaviour was rather strange, the truth came out.

He had been arrested for breaking a police officer's arm and with the thought of court, he decided to leave his troubles behind. Mum was angry, she said to him to leave. Then, he stormed into his car and that is when…'

### People.
My mind suddenly clouded over so grey, so dull, as the striking sound of a bullet shot Zero dead. Our pride lion shot dead for a few thousand dollars.

### How can they do this?
So many years they had banned trophy hunting, not one skin was taken home for decorating.

So many years it was unnecessary to kill for money, not one gunshot sound echoed loud and unforgettably.

## How does it happen?

It wasn't just a case of sending my friend the money to save my little dog, he needed to be rehomed too and I only knew too well how difficult it was going to be for me. To see him once again and then have to give him away.

As much as I wanted to, thought and tried to, it was not possible for us to stay together. It was not possible for me to take him to university. No matter how hard it was, I knew it was the right thing to find him a better home.

And I had managed to do it! During his recovery, I had done all that I could do to make the rest of his life a better life. From an advertisement I had put up at the pet store in town, an elderly couple were to get in touch.

Their little dog had recently passed and they wanted to rescue another, and similar, in its memory. Of course, sensibly, they asked to meet first before agreeing to take my little dog on as their own but it was to be tough.

The distance was one thing but after the incident, and the surgery, I was told my little dog looked, to put it best, unfriendly, aggressive even. He was now severely scarred above his right eye and had stitches all over his body.

Though there were no choices, I had to take the chances given and hope for the best, just hope they would see beyond the physical and love him in his nature for all who he is; love him for the truth in his innocence, his life…

The guy kindly offered to take me there so that I could once again meet my little dog and finally take him home. I was so excited to see him, but I was also so very sad. It was sad to think of how this was all to actually happen.

It took almost four hours, the journey, and as we were to approach closer, my heart was to beat faster. I started to wonder if my little dog would even recognise me after the three years that had been since I was to leave him.

And I can remember arriving as the sun was shining. I went alone to the front door to give it a little knock and a little bark followed in sound, it was most definitely the little bark I knew. My friend answered, we hugged.

That is when my little dog came running around the corner all hyper with his tail wagging and his tongue flapping. He sprinted straight towards me before jumping up into my arms to give me the biggest lick on the face!

## Why does it happen?

He started to become an alcoholic again, I could see it was all going to change again. I could see it was not going to be good for anybody. Not him. Not her. Not me. It was only going to be a matter of time before I would have to move again. It was not like I could stay there. He would need his space. They would need their space. The couple. And just when I thought it to be almost home too. But I am not writing this one about me. I am writing it about them. It was heart-breaking to see. To see both of them fall apart.

They were both so smart. They had great jobs. They had great characters. They had great personalities — kindness, compassion, understanding, love. Both of them. And from all of the people I was to know I would have thought those were the two who could get through, to manage getting themselves together and helping one another but no, it was not going to be. At least not while I was there unfortunately. He was spiralling and she was hardly surviving with the changes in his personality and behaviour.

### Is it not what they are to want?

The fire burns
My back turns
Away from you
I don't want to

### I hate it but I cannot help it.

I couldn't be happier for her, for them. My sister is getting married today, to a man that I can honestly say is a great man. He has been there for my sister far more than anybody else has, since our mother was to pass away.

If it was not for him, I do not know who my sister would've had to support her. To be there for her. As I've expressed it all already, it was not to be me. And I am still to feel guilty, I can't shift this horrible feeling I am to have.

Even though the relationship between us has become much closer to how I would like it to be, not completely but most definitely better than it was, I cannot be myself around her. It is like I am made to hold something back.

### It is your choice.

It was the first time I was to see my father again, at the wedding. It had been a little over two and a half years since he had evicted me, making me homeless. How careless. I can remember first seeing him at the bar before walking down to the church. I had wanted to buy a drink. I can remember taking the change out of my pocket when a coin had fallen to the ground.

My father had rushed over to pick it up and although he probably didn't mean it in the way that I had took it, I had wanted to punch him so hard that he wouldn't get back up again. It had reminded me, it had epitomised to me, his greed and his selfish nature. Only money, I didn't do it, of course. It was my sister's wedding and I was to promise myself this day was for her.

## My choice?

My sister had first asked me to give her away at the wedding but thought to change her mind once our father decided to come back into the picture.

## I am helpless.

I had to sit at the back of the church throughout the entire ceremony because I couldn't stop crying. It was like I had been holding back every public tear until this moment. I just couldn't stop. I was blubbering like a baby for the best part of an hour. I am not even joking, everybody started looking over at me, probably wondering why I seemed so upset about my sister getting married. But I wasn't! I was honestly so happy for them both.

It just took it out of me, it all seemed to be so surreal again. To be in the same place with this happiness for my sister yet still remember the sadness that had been before, of our mother. For our mother not being able to be here, to be next to me celebrating the joy for her daughter and I know we are still both to be so proud. I know it so. At least she was once able to meet this great man who is wanting to love my sister just as much as we both do.

**You are wrong.**

We did talk to each other that day. Well, after I had downed a few drinks and went over to talk to him, it didn't seem like he was going to talk to me.

People very rarely change, do they? The coward. Even though I did resent him, I had also forgiven him a long time ago. It was no good for me not to.

Though I had wanted to know why he couldn't talk to me in person when he decided to make me homeless. Why couldn't he just talk to me and fair?

He had no answers, my father, and it didn't surprise me whatsoever. Yet, I continued to make peace with him and even proposed to start over again.

We exchanged phone numbers and agreed to get in contact in a few days' time, to talk this through properly and make amends to our relationship.

**Are you right?**

Is a good friendship not based on the principle of being free to be yourself?

**What do you want?**

It got to a point when I knew it was bound to happen.

What are you talking about?

The guy. He has just admitted to me something which changes everything.

Did he tell you that he has feelings for you?

It is not even funny.

I am not trying to be.

Of course, you are not.

Is it a problem that he has turned to you and expressed these emotions?

Yes! It is a problem!

Tell me why it is a problem...

Because even though I may had thought it myself, I did not want to know!

Why would you not, is it not something to be a good thing?

He has a partner of seventeen years! And I am to see him as a brother!

So, you are not to feel the same?

You are joking, right?

I do not joke about love.

You are definitely joking...

Really?

I am not even gay for Christ's sake!

Now, I think you are the one trying to be funny...

Oh God...

Are you going to tell me what happened then?

The guy wanted to meet up on a Sunday. We do not even work on Sundays.

I know.

He drove me to the middle of nowhere in his van, to talk to me in private.

Go on.

When we stopped, it looked as though he was going to have a breakdown.

The van?

No, him!

Oh dear.

It was pretty uncomfortable for me. I kind of guessed what this was about.

How were you to guess?

Because I could feel it.

How could you feel it?

How am I supposed to know?

Well, did you ever lead him on?

No! I made sure to be platonic.

Did you ever want to then?

What do you think?

Do you want me to be honest?

I am not entirely sure!

Tell me what happened!

The guy turned around to me and then was to tell me he was to love me!

How did you respond?

I had said to him that I was to appreciate his feelings though I am not gay.

What was to happen after?

I was to leave the van and walk.

Was it not a long way to get home?

Not in comparison to the distance now between us.

What are you to mean?

Our friendship is never going to be the same again, is it?

## I want to be able to accept.

I don't know how many years it took for me to finally be able to let her ashes go and blow away into the wind which was to carry across the fields.

## It is not what I think it is.

It was a hard thing to do but I did, I had messaged my father and asked if he would like to meet up with me. However, unfortunately, he did not respond back for two months and his excuse was complete bullshit!

# Chapter Ten

**This journey.**

Five years have gone since my mother passed away, have gone since my sister ran away, have gone since I was left to fight against the day I did not want to live any more, the day all I had wanted was to somehow disappear.

**This pain.**

I remember the man once telling me that I wouldn't get anywhere in life without him, and there is a part of me which thinks he was actually right.

**This madness.**

The solitude of his time provides incessant thoughts which race around his mind so kind. 'Scenarios of peace or scenarios of chaos, which is greater?' He is to ask himself before the numbness creeps in and ceases over.

**This loneliness.**

Christmas is one to be celebrated with those you are to hold dear though it has become very much clear that I can no longer enjoy Christmas any more.

**Just give me some way out!**

I couldn't remember much until the next day when I woke

up with my head face down into the pillow like a lead balloon, all heavy and helpless.

I was to find myself with my clothes on and I had not quite made it into bed but at least the house which, for me, seemed to be a good enough effort.

My brain pounded somewhat loud and although I had pretty much become used to it, I really did not enjoy it, so I had downed a glass of water.

My stomach churned and grumbled something sick as I knocked back the cold but clouded water into my already poisoned, not best pleased, body.

I know that it isn't good for me, I'm not fucking stupid, but I do it anyway because who is really to care? I mean, is it not easier for me to forget that?

I know how angry I can become about it, it was only last night I had trashed up the streets of Canterbury all alone at a time I cannot remember.

My fury just takes over me and I go utter fucking crazy! All I can say is that I was fucking lucky nobody was around to see me otherwise... Christ!

My madness is something I can't always control! No, it is the drinking that I can't always control but, shut up, I have to drink because I need to forget!

## Can't you see?

I can remember her being so desperate
More desperate than anybody I had ever seen before

I can remember her talking to me
Telling me she had been beaten, abused and ignored

I can remember her breaking my heart
Breaking my heart because there was nothing I could do

## In all my hopeless attempts.

There was a poster put up on the front door to our university halls depicting Kilimanjaro and a large sum of money which, as I had read further, needed to be fundraised for a charity working with children in poverty around the world. Of course, this was something to have caught my attention, with the experiences in Egypt, Uganda and South Africa still very much with me and knowing first-hand just how different, just how difficult life can be for those who are living in these harder environments.

I had started to realise within myself that I, in ways similar but no doubt the same, related to others who happened to be struggling in and with life. It was becoming clear to me that if I had purpose, if I had reason to be and to live as myself, it was because I had wanted to give myself to what we may call 'God'. And by God, I do not mean so much in a religious sense but by God within everything, the something, whatever you wish to give it name, which makes the entirety of the world worth living for — for you and others.

It was a few days later I had managed to get involved in the project and, with the numbers who were to show to the first meeting, it resulted that if we could each fundraise around two or so thousand pounds, we would hit the charity's target. However, the projected target would not only go to the children who are in need of the money but it was also to cover the cost of the fundraising challenge as well — climbing Kilimanjaro in Tanzania… And I must admit, at first, there was an awful lot of controversy over this.

I had decided to fundraise the money not only by climbing the mountain, the highest mountain in Africa, which was going to be something pretty special if I am to be honest, but also by taking on a challenge back here in England too. And by already having success with the forty miles to Big Ben little escapade not so long ago, I had felt the urge this time to cycle around the perimeter of the Isle of Wight in the fastest time it was possible… for me. Although, to start with, I had to see if it was possible to get hold of a bike…

## In all that I have been given.

Over the past five years, I have come to sympathise an awful lot with the homeless, the people who live out on the streets with no place and no one to go back to, to talk to, to return knowing sweet solitude is available away from the wars of life. Over the past five years, I have come to notice it is those with continuous hardship and struggle who are most often the people ignored and forgotten, blamed and rejected; they are to be the people who are made to feel most guilty in our so-called fairest society. Over the past five years, I have come to know and more so be a part of this unpleasant experience but I have been one of the fortunate, fortunate to have always found somebody, more or less, to let me have a roof over my head at night.

## I am sick.

In the head. I am sick. In the head.
I wake up. I feel dead. In my head. I feel dead.
Out of bed. I can't get. Out of bed.
The light hurts. Eyes burn red. Out of bed. Eyes burn red.
Thoughts I dread. Get away now. Thoughts I dread.

In my mind. I have said. Thoughts they'd dread. I have said.

I was misled. I don't know. I was misled.

Go to hell. Straight on ahead. Was I misled? Straight on ahead.

## I need saving.

I am not entirely sure what persuaded me to do it more, but whatever the real reason is to be I am appreciative of the experience and it is something I do not think I will forget anytime soon, not this time spent with the poor.

Anyway, I had not anywhere to stay in honesty, so with that in mind, we were all actually to be in the right place, one could say, on this very unusual, yet rather memorable Christmas day, all festive, cheerful and happy. It wasn't very happy, if I am to speak truthfully. When I first walked in nobody wanted to tell me anything and it was hard to find somebody who would even look to see if I was genuinely interested in them.

As a person, as a human though, I tried not to take this to heart because I knew this was only what they were used to, they did not know what to do or who to trust and nor could I blame them, as I would be exactly the same.

If I was in their shoes, with no idea how to start over again, and not just in a materialistic way, but with the pain. The pain is by far the hardest thing to let go of and move on from, but that is not always seen as important in reality. Which is a shame, because the way I look at them and the question I want to ask you is, 'How on earth did they ever end up in a situation as bad as this?' Why on earth was there nobody there to help them?

I mean before now, and I don't mean to offer them an

allowance of a couple of pounds a week, or a place to stay for one night at a time if they are to behave. I am to mean find out how on earth did they ever end up here?

In a situation as this because it is a disgrace to ourselves, a disgrace that our values are focused more towards what we can see and not that we can feel. Do you feel good knowing there are people who live in your society who are down on their knees begging, not for your money but for your being? Your being, being able to understand who they are and how they are no different to you, but their experiences have been different.

Their experiences which have led them here in this homeless shelter where I am trying my best to make them feel not guilty, not different, not disconnected, but good — good for being alive and a part of life.

Good with belief there is not one person who is without purpose, without hope, without love. The problem is, what real difference can I make on my own? Quite possibly, something decent to a fair few, but they really need you too. They are to need us and, we all so often and far too easily forget, we are to need us. So, please let us not forget and please let us not hide because there is more to life than what is seen only on the outside.

**I need you.**

The Arch Bishop of Canterbury came to visit with his funny-looking hat and full-on attire to present us all with a most splendid Christmas dinner.

**You need me?**

Each day we wake up only to put on our masks which opposes waking up.

**To be different.**

My eyes blurred
Mind is disturbed
There is nowhere
For me out there

**To be me.**

Inevitably, I was always going to end up doing some, or dare I say many, drugs… probably. And it was not down to peer-pressure or anything, I had just wanted to be able to escape as far away as I really, possibly could go…

**Why?**

There was another guy who I had considered a great man and was to also help me throughout the harder times of my younger years. He was a man of strong, individual character who very much reminded me of somebody else with his hair long and his demeaner stern, by always going against the norm, against the conventional, and everything else all too serious in life, everything else all too boring for those who really, truly want to live.

He was to come across both in appearance and personality as a bit of a pirate and would you believe that the pirate actually had a boat? Yeah! We would go out sailing on it during the summer, across the English Channel and south to the islands of Alderney and Sark and it was just the best escapism! To go down there, to get away from the average every day. It really was to make me feel like I was in a film, or a dream, or something.

**To understand.**

In the darkness, orange and purple hexagonal shapes floated around me as time felt eternal and space was difficult to tell. I was sitting on a chair holding onto a balloon, the same chair and balloon I had been with when taking-in an awful number of drugs over the few hours before and fuck, fuck was I made to feel guilty... I mean, really guilty. I was told it was to be my eternity! Honestly, I had thought it a punishment for being so stupid, for thinking I was able to escape so easily, by not taking life too seriously...

It was horrible, there was nothing I could do! I had felt so fucking stupid... I was then to project out from the chair, to look back at myself still sitting on the chair just looking completely pathetic — slumped over all weak and helpless. What a waste of life... what a fucking waste of life I had thought. And worse, I was aware. I was conscious of what I had done! I had to accept how I was to be condemned but the thing is, I did accept — I had escaped... That is exactly when I came back feeling all hazy, thankful in my reality.

**What is it that you see?**

How fucked up was I to be sprawled around a toilet for three days straight, throwing up nothing but the green and yellow bile out from my stomach and sad, how sad must I have looked to anybody else left around to see me?

**I do not see sadness.**

I don't know what was put into the smoke but I was higher than a kite for the whole day long and it was beautiful. I had not a thing to worry about.

**Why are you so strange?**

The stand made hot drinks and pancakes and I really cannot say what drugs I had been taking that day, but there I was, just watching them flipping the mix all professional and everything whilst waiting for my coffee, thinking it will make me a little more lively, when suddenly I was to look up to see the people had pancakes for heads... pancakes for heads! With faces! The people had become pancake people! Of course, I had cried out loud in laughter... They had started to do this dance with their pans in one hand and their spatulas in the other, banging away to the rhythm of the night so jolly but fierce too... I had never seen anything so ridiculous in all my life! It was hilarious. Well, until I was to look back into the pans they were using to see their heads to be the ingredients they were mixing!

**Please tell me what you are to think about this...**

Okay, this was most definitely a combination of different drugs taken within a short period of time though I must tell you, it was fucked up.

So fucked up I don't advise anyone to do it. Although who am I to tell you what to do? Everybody has the right to do as they want to no, do they not?

Let's think about it. Anyway, I had become a new creator of the famous cat and mouse chase, the children's cartoon, in a somewhat subconscious state.

And it completely sucked! I was creating these fantastic sketches, these full-length seasons packed with drama and comedy at a rate unknown to man.

But every time I had lost consciousness something terrible would happen in the story: a character would somehow depict itself as somebody I knew.

My mother, my father, my sister, the man, a friend, whoever it was they would be killed off and guess who the bloody murderer was... it was me!

## I can see truth.

I have come to realise that I have a lot of anger inside of me, so much anger that I am sometimes scared of who I can be, if someone was to do something which upsets me I will flip utter fucking crazy, punch them, beat them, turn them black and blue or even possibly kill them, maybe.

No, no that is not me, it is only a vision in my head that I can see, yet all so very clear I have to choose who I really want to be, can I blame anybody else for the ways that I have turned out to be utter fucking crazy? I cannot because I am not, only if I want to be then it will be credible for you to see.

## Do you think I can act irrationally?

I am going to quit.

Quit what?

University.

For what reason?

Lack of interest.

Lack of interest?

It doesn't really challenge me.

Really?

Not in the ways that I was hoping it would.

And in what ways were you hoping it would?

I'm not sure but I saw it as the last opportunity to save myself.

Save yourself?

After everything, I could only envisage myself getting as far as university.

And then?

University would be able to provide everything I was to need for the future.

It doesn't?

To me, it seems to be more of a have-to than it is a want-to.

How do you mean?

It is all false advertising and false promising, false product and false hope.

Explain this to me.

The work, the teachers, the establishment; to me it portrays a lack of care.

A lack of care?

Besides money, I'm not sure anybody would see the purpose of being there.

But we need money in order to support a living!

Then please tell me, what exactly are we living for?

## All so very passionately.

Unfortunately, even though I had raised the money, I couldn't actually go to Tanzania to climb Mount Kilimanjaro. You see, without having any stability whilst I was to spend some time away from university, I could not afford to take the time off from work, nor was I able to afford the equipment and everything else necessary to take with me. Still, I was to donate all of the funds to the charity despite that I was, at the time, to be in over two grand of debt myself. However, I was to importantly remember that one thousand pounds of it saved my little dog, who is now very happy.

**Then tell me something.**

To be in nature makes one consider their purpose and importance in life.

**What is nature?**

Sleeping became a problem
I didn't want to sleep
I didn't want to let go of my mind
Perhaps I was scared
I didn't want to dream
I didn't want to free my brain to find
Down in dark unconsciousness
I didn't want to be
I didn't want to see and leave reality behind

**What is real?**

Mum? The voice inside my head was my mum. Where did you just come from? Was her voice real when it was only me walking under that big, bright sun? Where on earth have you been? I had asked with a tear in my eye. I have missed you, mum. But another voice in my head, why let myself believe in another lie. I cannot believe that you are talking to me! How stupid am I to be sure of something that I cannot see? Are you here with me now, say, where are you to be? Yet, there I was, out in the fields we once walked together, with my very wonderful mother: the voice of me.

**What is true to you?**

I am absolutely fucking done
There are no words I can say

All I want is a gun
To put myself down and out of this misery
Because it is he, the devil, who has won

# Chapter Eleven

**I.**

And here
I
stand, moved in such
a way
I
cannot describe

God
has blessed
me,
has reduced
me
to something

so small,
so big
I
cannot understand:
I
am not alone

I
never have been
and in all this time

I
have tried to deceive
faith

God
has only made
me
believe more:
there is
only now

I
am starting to know that
I
am experiencing something which
I
cannot escape from and…

I
am so
thankful to
remember it
can only
be this way.

## I can create anything.

You cannot create a colourful picture if you are only to
have black ink.

## Me?

A good friend of mine had called to say he was getting

married to a girl from America and if it was at all possible, for me to attend their wedding out in Minneapolis, Minnesota. Well, I had never been to the USA before and I had not wanted to miss his wedding, albeit we were only just turning twenty-one at the time and the thoughts of his naivety had crossed my mind, that's for sure. But this was to happen simultaneously with my thoughts on leaving university, and it all went together rather conveniently because it was then I had a valid reason, a valid excuse, to quit and find work to save up the money to accept the invitation which I really could not ignore. In consideration and with respect, he was one of my good friends, one of my best friends, with whom I had shared many experiences throughout our school years and, of course, to always remember, Uganda.

**Never.**

    Gardener, kitchen porter, building labourer

    Car cleaner, checkout operator, restaurant waiter

    Painter and decorator, take-away deliverer, café barista

    Cocktail bartender, I'm sure there is another, imagine if it was forever?

**Why would I believe you?**

    When quitting university, I had to find someplace else to stay and, after several months of not talking to each other, the guy and I were to finally resume friendship and put all of our differences behind us. He was to tell me the year before was rather difficult for him and with much of the stress from work, along with a few other things, his thoughts and feelings were somewhat chaotic. Although what he had said before was true, he was to no longer feel the same and that he was now happier than ever.

With this having been said, I had thought it was a good idea to move on and finally, once again, be friends. We were, before all of that, very good friends and I had missed the times we had spent together because, like I have mentioned previously, he was like a brother to me. We were to meet up in London for the usual day-off, bar to bar drinking, drinking and talking about all things ridiculous, and that was when I had asked if it was possible to stay with him for a few months until I headed for America.

**Why would you want to?**

It is quite an important skill to have, to feel comfortable enough in yourself to allow yourself to be able to rest, even sleep, in any given place.

**There is so much I do not understand.**

I have always wanted to travel the world ever since I was a little boy. I can still remember sitting in my treehouse at the back of our garden, I must have only been about four or five years old, and these thoughts appearing:

1. Is it possible for me to be able to touch upon all of the land on earth?

2. I feel as though I have been here before, I know there is something more.

3. Why, I don't know, think I am connected to Native American Indians?

These thoughts have always stuck with me throughout my life. For most of the time I will only laugh and joke about them with others, with friends, yet looking back I have started to wonder just how was I ever to have them?

**And I try so hard.**

Five jobs I was working at one time, five! Some days I would work up to three different jobs from eight or nine in the morning until two or three the following, only then to sleep a little and wake up to do all it all again!

**What am I doing?**

I was only to know what I had wanted; I was only to know what I could do.

**This is mad!**

I had to do it. I had to go! And I will tell you this, it was one of the best things I have ever done. Having saved up enough money, I had decided to purchase a ticket to San Francisco and a return from New York with only myself to find a way across. I had in mind a few things, a few places that I should try and visit but, I guess, it was more a leap of faith. I do not know.

**Go!**

One hour to the airport, three hours there, eleven hours on the plane, another hour with a questionnaire, half an hour on a bus, and another half an hour to walk, a little time to find something to eat, and I made plenty of time for strangers to talk, twenty minutes at the reception, one hundred and twenty to get ready, I had to be quick because I needed to drink but only because the hostel was not at all taking it steady, eight hours out on the town, so many people from places all over, the welcome was worth over a million dollars... this was the beginning of my supernova.

**Open your eyes.**

The first few days, all I had wanted to do was wander around alone. It was incredibly peaceful. I had taken a map with me, to be precautious, though I was not looking at it. I was to enjoy letting each street take me wherever I had needed to go. And strange though it sounds, there were times, when no person was to be near, it felt as though I could've been somebody from here.

**What do you see?**

San Francisco, I know, is a place of wonder, of beauty, of space. A space to free your mind like those in past times like Haight-Ashbury, the swinging sixties, and before in nineteen-thirty, when a few had the idea to build a bridge so spectacular over the Golden Gate Strait. It amazed me. I had spent some time down at Pier 39 and looked out to Alcatraz, imagine, and I had roamed the streets of the city, which all looked so pretty, with its modern art of big heart alongside people playing sweet music to the sound of jazz.

Then I was to head down to L.A, the city of angels they say. I was to see how amazing it looked with its bright light shining up into the sky at night and the Hollywood sign standing so tall. It really is quite powerful. Many of the houses are more to be like mansions, and there were things that passed by which caught my eye only because they shouted a million dollars. I had taken a walk over the stars of fame and stopped at the ones in which I remembered their name. How nice it must be to be remembered.

San Diego, I know, is a place where I had wanted to stay for much longer to have much more fun. I had wanted to stay because I can remember the day when I went down to the old town which is so very vibrant in colour and in sun. It had a feel of something I could almost touch in memory. Though, when thinking about it, the thoughts were to very quickly leave me, but I was in no need to worry because I had soon enough found some friends to find Belmont Park before the horizon set the perfect image dark.

Then we went on together to find some place other where the fun was to be had. And it is so that I must add that I had absolutely no idea this even existed in North America. When once working in a bar I was told by a man, who very much looked like Albert Einstein, 'the United States is the best of all God's garden' and, without experience, I was not totally fine just to believe in his words. However, some time later, when I had raced up a sand dune on my way to Arizona and thought over all I had seen so far...

And already, Phoenix. By the time I had got to Phoenix I was to feel like a new person, a free person by which, I mean, I could be me. The United States of America — the land of opportunity had given me the opportunity! To celebrate, a group of us went out for some food, real spicy, and while the girls shared a cocktail, the guys shared a beer. Well, of course, with all the cheer necessary, it did not take long really before we had found ourselves at a bar because after we had a taste of the chilli, we had turned pretty silly!

There is no stopping them, the people there. They're crazy! But beautiful. We continued on up to the Grand Canyon and I had thought what to expect, I had seen pictures, though it is not until you are there that you can truly respect just how grand, just how inspiring it really is. There laid a sign which part read 'some tribes call the canyon home' and it was then I had said, to myself, 'I think I know something more.' We adventured on the path which took us below and I am sure never to have felt so peaceful.

What is an American road trip without a little fun in the unreal? It's a must do — have to — yes — you. Will you get yourself to Las Vegas? How mad can a place really get to be? Everything is so big, so bright, so impressive; the hotels are massive, the fountains exciting, the replicas compelling. And the casinos, well, who knows, a chance to place down some good luck? If you want to, that is. It does not matter, all which has been said before and all that has been seen until now, unless you've experienced it for yourself!

Where better to shrug off a hangover than in a place named Death Valley? Scorching heat, salty plain, burning feet, the devil got me ball and chain. He did, no really. Mama, help me! This lasted all of ten minutes because it was then the temperature had basically, not that I can explain scientifically... evaporated all the alcohol out of my weak and weary body. To admit the truth, I had felt elevated. I was again able to sense out, to soak up a scenery so powerful in its presence and permanence bigger than man.

And sometimes I can and, sometimes, I cannot remember all the places that I have been and all the places that I have forgot. When another is driving I am most likely staring, straight out of the window, glaring into the sun, reflecting down shining brightly upon everything except that in shadow, because it has not yet begun to give it beauty, one must wait its turn, only too much will be too much and too much will eventually burn. It is all in time and patience is key, to look out of the window there seems a mystery.

Yosemite. I have never, in all my life, this life, seen

something closer to what I have dreamed to be paradise. Nature has never failed to impress me. I have seen some pretty wonderful things back in Europe, out in Africa, here in America, but I think, and I was star-struck by the Grand Canyon, Yosemite has topped it all. I haven't even a word better than beautiful. It is beautiful! I was to wander the little paths through to where the giant sequoia trees grow alongside streams of water, across the mountain top in flow.

San Francisco, I know, is somewhere I have been before. 'Though, before I have been and to all that I have seen I am still keen to come back and see some more.' So, with a friend I had returned and together we shared a great time on a boat under the bridge with each, in our hands, a glass of white wine. Though my memory is somewhat hazy, I can remember the weather was kind of too, the usual San Francisco fog was not enough for us to stop, even if it had turned the sky grey from the brighter colour of blue.

San Jose, Santa Cruz, Monterey to name a few, Big Sur, Pismo Beach, Malibu and L.A again too. What a road trip! What an adventure! It really is quite something when you are to put yourself out there, to see where life will take you if you are to let it. Throughout this time travelling, I had thought to myself repeatedly 'this is money I could have saved, money I could have put towards my future, money I could have put towards a deposit on a house if sensible' just how well spent this money really was.

**No, no way.**
It was in L.A. I had heard a sound. A sound that I knew. A sound that I can remember. A girl was playing it. She was playing it in her room. She had left her door open. I was

walking past on my own. I had asked if it was okay for me to come in. I had asked if it was okay for me to listen. It was the sound of the guitar. It was the words that were sung. It had taken me back to a place. A place I knew of so well. If only. I wish you were here.

**No, it cannot be.**

I took a ride over to Minnesota for the wedding and, strange though it sounds, it had felt like I was leaving something behind. Something that I did not want to. Something that I could have called home. But I had to go.

It was great to see my friend again though, it had been almost a couple of years since we were to last see each other. He was to be in Russia when I in South Africa and it was then after I had gone away to study at university.

We were to catch up, have fun, but I could not keep it in mind that he was just about to get married and to get married already. I had not even met his fiancée up until. However, I knew my friend and I trusted his decision.

The wedding was pretty special, although very Christian. I had really appreciated being a part of it and I was to really like her as a person. I am sure she is who he had been looking for and I am so very happy for them.

**It is up to you.**

I didn't stay for long after the bride and groom had left the wedding. It just wasn't the right scene for me, not really. I had wanted to get back out there on the road again. I had just wanted to be on my own again and travelling.

**All of it.**

Minnesota. Wisconsin. Illinois. Indiana. Michigan. Ohio.

Pennsylvania. New York. New Jersey. Maryland. Washington D.C. Gettysburg. Niagara Falls. Vermont. New Hampshire. Massachusetts. Connecticut. Manhattan.

## What do you want?

If I am going all the way to the USA then I must try my best to see as much of the land as it is possible and seek out every opportunity that I can take.

## What is home?

Is there no greater freedom than the freedom of imagination? Of not knowing where you are and where you are going to, of who, when, why, what? And, of course, in all of this, how, how do we have imagination?

## Think about it.

Is it me
Is it us
Who is to
Owe the world?
Is this not
How we are
Who we are
Think about it
Why would I
Why would you
Even think to
Owe the world?

## Have you ever not known what you're able to do?

Life. Like seriously, life just continues to amaze me each

day to the next. Remember back when I couldn't go to Tanzania to climb Mt. Kilimanjaro? Well, the charity had called me to say that, instead, I could go to Morocco. Go to Morocco and climb the highest peak in North Africa, Mt. Toubkal. Going along with another university would give me this new opportunity. They had said if I was to need more money, they would give me more time. I really could not believe it. I was going to actually climb up a mountain! The charity had thanked me for my contribution and for my hard work. I thanked them and said 'it's my pleasure'. I'm sure to do it sometime again. So, I went and I spent a month in Morocco like you could never believe. I had topped Toubkal, trekked the Sahara, visited Essaouira, Marrakesh, Fez and Casablanca. And all I can really do is appreciate her, my mother.

# Chapter Twelve

**Like a mystery.**

Girls man, girls. I have been one of the lucky few to share with so many. Every girl each has something about them which gets me going mad, crazy. They are all beautiful, all of them, you know, not one of them is ordinary. And I cannot forget any… It is impossible yet so beautiful though so hazy.

**It seems as though.**

Most of my dreams are complete and utter madness. Fantastic, bonkers and strange. Seriously, there are mornings when I am to wake up thinking that I have not yet been to sleep, that I have been elsewhere, that I am beyond tired from all of the travelling and exploring I have been doing, enduring.

I am always meeting again people from my past. My mother, my father, my sister a few times, the man, several old friends that I once used to have. No dream has ever been the same but sometimes I am to dream out different scenarios of the same thing, almost like searching out for different answers.

**When teaching us.**

I had thought it was best to go back and finish university, to have a degree was going to help me in the future. At one time, I was considering to try and change my course. However, without finance, it was impossible to fund an extra two years.

Having already completed two was the problem as the funding paid three, it meant that I was left with no choice about it, really.

Although the third year was not to be so bad in honesty, a class that I was to study dealt with notions of utopia. Dystopia also but I was to enjoy our head of department's teaching. I guess he really was the only lecturer to capture my attention. He knew something that was more than the usual regurgitation of opinion — unlike others he was interesting and had intent...

### We pretend not to know.

There are so many people I have not said anything about, nothing. Sometimes, when it is good, very good, I find it enormously difficult to.

There is a friend of mine, we have known each other since we were ten. Sometimes I, and now I have, just want to tell her how much I love her.

### Why?

I honestly don't know the truth in this.
I think last night somebody had punched me.
They had punched me in the face, twice.
Both times I was knocked to the floor.
Both times I had gotten straight back up.
They were angry about something I had done.
I cannot remember anything I could have done.
I would have done to upset him, them.
They were more in numbers and in height.
Both factors against me, why would I fight?
Both factors against sense, it doesn't make sense.
They punched me and beat me for what?

**Why do we act as if we do not know?**

When we meet somebody, anybody, the first thing we do, and without realisation, is to try and understand who they are and who they are to us.

**You know the brightest lights can knock you over.**

It was only sometime before I had this amazing night in Central London watching the fireworks shoot over Big Ben and the Palace of Westminster. It was certainly a great time to remember, being with a couple of friends I had met in South Africa and, with me, a girl I knew from university who happened to be one of the most beautiful girls I was ever to have fallen for.

She was a girl from Constanta, Romania, and I shall not speak too much of her because sometimes, and it really does not matter how hard you will try to, you cannot keep hold onto the things you want most. You just can't. And perhaps in time there is reason why but until then, and if when, it is most probably best to move on, let go and forget all she had meant to me.

So, it was, only sometime after, that I had this awful night in Canterbury with another friend I was to have in company and only because we were both to be so lonely. We had decided to spend the New Year's Eve together, we had thought to try and make the most out of the occasion like we are supposed to do. You know, celebrate and commemorate the year through…

But for us, well at least for me, this was not to be the case because I had only loneliness to look back upon. And when I am to talk of loneliness, I do not mean there is nobody to be around me. Fortunately, there is most often somebody to be around me, yet that is not to say I am not to be lonely. To be lonely is to function like a stranger in a world which does not know.

My friend and I had dressed up, gone out, messed about and drank to the point which we had almost forgotten what we were actually to be doing together in the first place. However, it is when I drink, I tend to lose my temper, I am soon to become angry, I turn into somebody I do not want to be, I do things which are stupid, I walked in front of a car, he saved me.

### Are we, am I, not strong enough?

It was strange, because before it happened, I had been thinking about him an awful lot, the man that is. I had been thinking about him so much that I had started writing down all these things to try and make sense of it.

It was then, after writing down all of these things, I had thought to rest by listening to music and trying my best to forget the world, if only for a little while, when my phone flashed and a photo appeared on the home screen.

It was of him. It was of us together at a football match taken many years ago. We were to look pretty happy in each other's company. The man was to send me this photo even though we had not talked once since I had left?

### And you know to have strength is a choice.

The thing is that I had thought I was to be doing all right at the time. Okay, I was not thinking that I was to be in paradise, or to be following my dream as such, but at least I was to be relatively content in the idea of moving on. I had started to realise that moving on from the past was now necessary for me, that it is not fair for me to continue carrying this huge, heavy weight of guilt around all of the time. I mean, what was I doing with it anyway? Good? It was good to practice the idea of letting everything go to be honest, to not think of blaming myself for all that had happened.

The thing is that I had thought I was to be doing all right at the time. Okay, I was not thinking that I had suddenly dealt with all of my problems, that I had managed to forget all of my troubles and life was to be all hunky-dory and soon to be great again. No, no way. That would be a terrible idea to have, would it not? Perhaps I did not know it so because I was only to know what it was like to feel like shit. It does not take a genius then to figure out which method I had taken to try and turn my dreaded thoughts, which have stagnated my mind, into a space of freedom in what is present.

The thing is that I had thought I was to be doing all right at the time. Okay, I was not thinking that I could be so stupid to let this happen again, to do the same thing as when I was fifteen years old and had wanted to escape, escape as far away as I could possibly get. I don't know. How did I possibly let this happen again? I was found lying unconscious in the middle of the high street in Canterbury, apparently. I can only remember waking up in hospital, not knowing where I was and attached to all sorts of apparatus. The doctor: he was not impressed. He had said I was very lucky to be there.

## Pink Floyd.

They were there for me when nobody else was to be there for me.

Their sound comforted me when there was nobody else there to comfort me.

Their lyrics spoke to me when there was nobody else there to speak to me.

They were there for me when nobody else was to be there for me.

## Thank you.

I had done it, I had finally made it through to the end of my institutional studies and I am pretty sure, no matter what, I am not going to do it again.

At least not for a while anyway because I hate the idea of doing that which society tells you; I am I and you are you and I will go my own way.

## You have always been strong enough.

My grades were never the best and I never expected them to be. Throughout all of my school days, there were only a handful of times when I could actually put the effort in which was required. Whether it was due to a lack in attendance because of one reason or another, or a lack in work because I was uninterested in the subject and the teaching perhaps, or a lack in my ability to truly understand what it was being taught did not matter too much. What mattered was the feeling of wasting an opportunity.

However, besides this, I had always made the grade which took me to the next step, even if it was only marginal. I had always done just enough to get myself through. During secondary school I happened to be in most of the top classes until my mother fell ill and other things started to fall apart as well. It was from then on, through to university, I had to put my education to one side and concentrate, well, dedicate the majority of my time towards other things, which made getting better grades very difficult.

That is not to say I didn't get good grades. I didn't do badly, considering. Considering that it was not until I had finished university when I was to first discover I have dyslexia. I had no idea! I had thought everybody was to read at a pace similar to me, to make many spelling and grammar mistakes in their work like me, to not be able to maintain concentration… A lecturer of mine mentioned it once finishing my last assignment. It was only then I took it upon myself to get tested and, so it is, I am to be dyslexic!

### Take some time to realise this.

There are times when I want to celebrate without any reason to do so and there are times when I do not want to celebrate at all, even when there is.

I did not want to celebrate finishing university, nor did I want to attend my graduation later on either. For me, I did not achieve that I had wanted.

Not in terms of grades but in terms of finding out what it is I want to do, what I can do; where to go next; to have support, to be full of confidence.

I was eventually persuaded by a couple of friends to attend the graduation, and it was a great opportunity to invite my Gran to Canterbury Cathedral.

### Be around others who realise this.

She very much reminds me very similarly of the Queen of our country, my grandmother. She is my mother's mother and my words will only speak fondly of her because she is nothing but a whole bunch of everything to me and it is her I can call family because she, she has never let me down.

She, unlike the Queen of our country, does not have a lot of money, nor a place for me to stay, yet she has always tried her best to help me whenever she had an opportunity and it is without her, as there were occasions when I literally had nothing, I would have gone out and taken unfairly.

She, my grandmother who I love so much, did not only help me every now and again financially, but she is also one of very few people who has always allowed me to just be me, myself. And not once, so like my mother, has she told me to be anybody different; not once did she ask me to be anything other than myself.

**It can be hard.**

I was so lost
I had finished university
But had no home
Nowhere left to go

**To do it alone.**

Although I was fortunate enough most of the time, there were some nights when I had to face up to sleeping out on the streets in the lonely and cold.

**I once had to.**

The station was the same
When I had woken up
Sprawled out on the train
Not knowing much of anything
I had taken a ride
A ride to go home
Wherever home is to be

The journey is never far
Though it was not unusual
For me to fuck up
Not caring about anybody else
And doing too many drugs

**It was not good.**

It was a stupid thing to do and it was only my own fault for it happening. I was absolutely wasted, I mean, I could hardly walk. I was basically crawling beside the entrance to London Victoria train station, at a time something around four o'clock in the morning, when two men approached me and asked if I was to be all right. I was not able to say I was all right, that is when they had grabbed both of my arms back and propped me upright.

At that moment, I had realised they were not there to help me but instead take whatever they could from me. I had looked down to see one of them trying to take my phone out of my jean trouser pocket. Of course, anybody would, I had tried to push him away so he could not take it but I was physically held back by the other. It was then I had managed to shove over the other one holding me back. However, I was no longer to have my phone.

I should have then left it there though I was angry, so I had chased them as far as I could and shouted aggressively at them to come back. That was a stupid thing to do. Both of them were about a foot taller than me, looked as though they were to belong to a gang of some kind and God had I known if they were to be carrying a knife or anything alike. They had turned around and headed back over, it is that I cannot properly remember but...

**I had thought life to be unfair.**

One weekend I had woken up in a pile of leaves by the side of the road on the Saturday and then Eton College on the Sunday... which, one could say, was experiencing the two different ends of the social scale! Although, to be visiting Eton was only because I had a friend who taught there. It is not like I had the privilege to be there otherwise. However, it is so that I do like to think what it would have been like to be privately educated in one of the more prestigious academic institutions though: Eton and then, perhaps, either the University of Oxford or Cambridge. Imagine what it is like to have the best opportunities, facilities, support, encouragement and respect...

**Think of Africa.**

You know where I am to go when times get too hard and feelings too low.

**Life may not always be what it seems to be.**

The English government support a project that has been going on for years and hopefully will continue to do so. The project is mostly volunteer based, encouraging many younger citizens to participate, and aimed to help achieve the United Nation's Millennium Development Goals, or, what are now the Sustainable Development Goals since the year of 2015. The project, I should say projects, expands across twenty different countries around the world and involves volunteers both, and in equal number, from the United Kingdom and the country which each project takes place.

The project is partly funded by the government yet those

who are from the United Kingdom do have to fundraise a fair amount of the money also, although it is not so much, unlike other fundraising and volunteer work I have done, where each person is set to go out alone and do everything by themselves, while the 'charity' holds back and waits to collect all of the hard work and reward. The project, in fact, works in a way which gives, as though it seems, with real intent. They are to provide a partnership with the volunteer from the start through to the end, even once returning home!

**You will see.**

To fundraise the money, I had decided this time to try and walk, with a little running here and there, the length of Hadrian's Wall. A distance covering, as the crow flies, they say, a great eighty-four miles coast to coast.

Even though, and most often it is better, I had support, I had thought to do the actual challenge of taking on the wall by myself. It was that I had wanted to not only do this project for the world but to also do it for myself.

I mean this in the sense that if I can keep on giving myself away to others, for others, the least I can do is find the strength to be able to give everything I give to myself as well. If not more, then I can continue giving.

Still not having much money, I had not much time to do it. So, with a total of four days away from work, I was to see how far I could make it across the famous Hadrian's Wall — including travel up to and down from the North.

Starting out west and heading east, I had covered around thirty-five miles on the first day of walking, leaving forty-nine for the second. I did not research but I had been told beforehand the eastern half was much easier.

At six o'clock in the morning and blessed in sunshine, I had again endured on with the trail which was, I must say to my astonishment, well signposted and directed, not to mention the abundance in its beauty even.

The entire trail was utterly incredible, I mean, astonishing, really. The diversity of the path had led me through all kinds of wonders and there were, at times, areas which, it seemed, were all just waiting, expecting me.

It felt as though I was standing on top of the world at one point high up. But if I did not think in such ways, it was like the world was just going to swallow me up to make up for the lack of appreciation and respect I had.

I was on to win with almost six hours of sunlight left and only twenty miles to go on mostly a flat surface. It was then I had decided to sit down, take a little rest and a bite to eat ahead of the finish I had thought best.

When standing back up, I had felt something not quite right in my ankle. Not wanting to fail, I had carried on for another two miles before I could no longer walk altogether. It was unfortunate but I was not able to finish.

However, more positively, I had collected a total not short of one and a half thousand pounds, which I was to donate to the project. The project being, which I have not yet mentioned, out in Tanzania, Africa. I am going back!

**I know that you care.**

I cannot believe I am going back.

I know, you are a very lucky guy.

I never did tell you much about South Africa.

Nor Egypt, Morocco and Uganda.

Well, Egypt, I was only a young child.

It was still to mean something to you though.

My family took me there.

And Uganda, the experience really changed you.

Uganda was difficult, finding out my mother had cancer again.

But there was something else you had also experienced.

You could say that. It is when I had first realised who I am going to be.

Uganda was difficult.

And I could not believe how unjust yet beautiful the world is.

Then why is it you were never to tell me about South Africa?

Because that is where I was able to let everything go.

You did not do that though.

How on earth do you know?

Because you cannot give it up.

What are you even talking about?

Everything that you are to want.

You think you are to know?

Believe me, I have always known that very something about you.

South Africa had given me the strength to go on. It brought life back to me.

Yet, you have gone on again only to try and lose it.

There is something in life which once you have it is impossible to lose.

**It means something to you.**

There were many of us on the project and I could not have been put into a better team. The project was to have a few different teams so that we could cover a much larger area of Tanzania. And our team, our team was family.

## Keep on trying.

We were there, in Tanzania, to try and help small-sized communities work in a way which may make their living an easier, more efficient and better pleasant experience, while conserving their own ideas and practices.

## Life will keep on giving.

We were to live with the locals of the village, two volunteers to each house. Apart from our house, in our house we were to have four. It was named the mad house and it was very much an appropriate name for it. We were to never know exactly how many people lived there. We had estimated twelve.

Not counting ourselves, it was an almost half Muslim, half Christian household and the village was pretty much one or the other actually when talking in terms of faith. It was never such an issue though. Everybody had respect regardless of their belief — unlike some other places I am to know!

Despite the fact it was considered to be in extreme poverty, the village was brought to life by the people, the people who every day carried a smile along with them if nothing else. I do admit to it being very basic though; only the better houses had a roof and all of the food was locally harvested.

There was no running water, well only to the pumps in the village centre and not all of the time was there to be water either. There was little to no infrastructure, hardly any electricity and no real place to be treated if ill. But the village did have character and we got to enjoy it for three months!

## We are all innocent.

The children of Africa are some of the happiest children I have ever seen.

## We are all to deserve better.

I am to say 'enjoy it' but this is not to say it was easy nor do I think of their situation in disrespect either. I am aware that although it was an experience for me, very much a challenging one, it was only to be a short experience. I was not them. I did not wear their shoes. I knew it was only short, momentary and eventually I would once again have an opportunity.

## All we have to do is to allow ourselves to be strong.

'Where are you going? Come on. Wait up. Mate, wait! I will come with you. You cannot go alone.' The village is in complete darkness. It is dangerous. 'Mate, come on.' The wild dogs howl while we are to walk across the village.

'What are you doing here?'

'Can you help me convince him to stay?'

'What?'

'He wants to leave.'

'What has happened?'

'Nothing. Leave it.'

'Come on man. Just say it.'

'Say what?'

'Tell her what you had told me before coming here.'

'Seriously?'

'Can we keep it down, they will hear us?'

'Can we go elsewhere?'

'Now?'

'We cannot stay here.'

'Where are we going to go at this time of night?'

'We can go and sit underneath that giant tree with the branch for a seat?'

'Good enough for me.'

'Yeah, okay then.'

'Good, we can talk it through there.'

'Are you really going to wear flip-flops for this?'

'I am not going back inside.'

'Be careful not to catch your feet on anything then.'

'Have you got cigarettes?'

We head down a path left, turn right, cross over a field, and then another. Turn left again, pass through the tall grass either side, and ahead, the tree. For half an hour we had sat down quite peacefully and sorted things out. There was laughter and our friend had completely forgotten about leaving. And it was also when we were all to hear a sound coming from behind us. The sound was like that of somebody standing on, and breaking a stick.

Then, immediately, he was sitting sideways on, our friend had jumped up. Totally in shock, he had started to run back down the path really quickly. As I stood, I could see objects being thrown at him and something running. It was a person. It looked like our friend was being chased, if not attacked. And I was then to see my other friend facing down, holding her head. Objects, I had no idea what, but I could hear them hit the floor, passed us. She was not moving and I could no longer see that which was happening.

Fight or flight? I had to run. I had to run. I had to run out from the tree in order to see. And I was hoping that she would follow me, but she just stayed there, still. I did not have a choice — our friend had gone. I had to go back and get her. Heading back towards the tree I ran as fast as I could without hesitation. There was no time for it. I grabbed her and pushed her out in front of me. Shouting at her, telling her to run as fast as she possibly could, 'Go, just go!'

I had stayed behind her, trying to protect her. Thinking that I was fucked. Thinking that at any moment I was to get something sharp into my back. Something heavy hitting my head, knocking me out. I took a sudden look. There were three at least, silhouetted figures, standing by the tree behind. Of course, I did not tell her until we had found a place safe for us to hide.

## And to allow ourselves to be forgiven.

We should not have been out at that time, we could only blame ourselves. We could have jeopardised the project, we should have been left for worse. We should not have thought to be superior, we could have thought better. We could, it was said, have been killed but we should not think in averse.

## We are all different.

The locals had said to us it was most likely an attack from the Maasai.

## That is how we work!

And it was without warning, eight wild dogs came running towards my friend and me. Three went around us left, three went around us right, two came straight through the middle and together they had us strategically surrounded with their jaws of gnashing teeth and their eyes of evil staring directly into ours. They knew how to attack, and again, how utterly stupid we were. It was also pitch black and we should not have been outside walking back at that time. Nobody else was to be around! In an instant, I had shouted to my friend, 'Get your back straight up against mine. Do not once turn around on me. Do not turn your back on them!' I had told him, shouted at him, 'We have to make ourselves as big and as loud as possible.' I had shouted, 'Do not attack them.' He had tried to kick one of them! I had told him, 'Whatever you do, do not fucking run. They will get you, and me.' The dogs would each take turns to try and pounce in towards our feet. I had guessed, if we were to kick back in defence, it would have given another dog an opportunity to grab a hold of one of our legs and then drag us down while another jumped up for the jugular. We were in a stand-off. Eight wild dogs, two British boys, and a minute of calculated action.

If it was not for the noise we had made and this house nearby responding by turning on some bright light and bashing together these pots and pans, I am not sure if I would be sitting here today, writing down this story to you.

**Ask, what is fundamental about you?**

When in Africa, I really do consider how truly amazing it is to be alive.

**What is it that keeps you alive?**

In the field, I sat alone, gazing up towards the stars and reflecting upon life. This figure approached me in the darkness, I could not make out much. They carried a stick and wore a cloth which was to wrap around the body. It was about ten metres away when they had stopped, then started to dance, some tribal type dance. I was completely freaked yet continued to watch. This rhythm he had, it was fascinating. Until he struck down his stick.

It was then when I had decided to run. I was not taking any more chances.

## Does life provide whatever you are to want?

When I had to return back to the UK, it was not OK. I had no place to go. Where I thought I would go, I could not go. However, I had Salmonella. Then I was to end up in hospital for a while because they thought Ebola. There had recently been an outbreak and I had just returned from Africa.

## And is it not for you, to find home?

Then I went on to Paris. A friend of mine, a girl I had met in Morocco, was studying there and had told me to go and stay with her. She was sweet, so kind, but unfortunately, I was pretty messed up. It did not work out between us with her studying and me not being able to speak French. To be honest, I could not have felt more lost in a place that is supposed to be so full of love and art and passion. Basically, I had to get up and leave again.

# Chapter Thirteen

**Thinking.**

Carl Jung — How can we, in one moment, be fully immersed within a memory and then, in the next, have thoughts that say the memory never existed at all?

**Feeling.**

I am now twenty-two and I still don't know what to do so I had better call a friend to see if he can lend a hand to help me out and see what is about.

**Intuition.**

I will tell you now, everything that I have written so far is all because of this I am about to write; if there is anything in life which has taught me…

**Sensation.**

I had called my good friend. The friend from school, Uganda, the wedding in Minneapolis, America. He had been there for me throughout most of my life in one way or another, so he was my best, sort of only, bet, to be honest.

He and his wife had moved to London, after spending much time in Russia and America doing various Christian missionary work together, so that he could pursue his dreams in becoming a certified church minister.

I have always supported him in his beliefs, even though I am not a religious guy myself. That is not to say I do not believe in God, though, just not in the same ways as any religion I have sought after and researched.

He had always respected both my perspective and thought, as I did his, which, I would say, was the true strength that brought our friendship through so many years. We believed in each other far more than we knew.

I had stayed, and I cannot thank them enough by the way, for a couple of months over the winter period before, and it was something like a miracle, I was to get a position as a photographer onboard a cruise ship in America!

**I have been left speechless.**

I have been asked many times before if I am to believe in love at first sight.

**Wow!**

The cruise ship was to have everything that I had wanted, everything that I could have dreamed of if dreams are such a thing. I can remember the first day when I had arrived; it was to feel like I had returned home in the sense that I was both excited and nervous. Excited because it was something I had needed, nervous because I did not believe it could be something true.

**There is nothing else I can say!**

If you love me
Then love me all that you can
Because if you do
You will never fear or be afraid

Of all the love
I have and want to give you

## Is it now that I can truly believe?

What I am to mean by everything is that everything is
actually the girl.

## I don't know what I can say!

I knew, from the very first time I was to see her, that I had
wanted to spend the rest of my life with her. I have no idea
from where but I knew this girl.

## God.

It was like I had been catapulted through the past, present
and future all at one time, flipped upside down, inside out, to
the left, to the right, back, forth, here, there, everywhere;
something happened to me I cannot explain!

## This means everything to me.

To describe her, I cannot. Not properly. She was the most
beautiful girl I have, and I mean this entirely, ever, ever seen
and the strangest thing happened to me when we were to look
into each other's eyes on that very first day I had got onto the
ship wanting so much to start my life anew.

## It is not me.

I have always been
Looking for you
And never did I see
To find you here

**There is only you.**

This girl, seriously. I can't get enough. How can she possibly be this perfect?

**Who is able to?**

But as God speaks
To stay true to myself
Guided by a light
I was found

**This is so true.**

It was her smile. Her smile is the best smile in this whole, entire world...

**Find the missing key.**

Not to be lost
In feelings I once had
Nothing like I feel now
Since I believe

**If I had listened it would have been so easy.**

Her voice, it got me.
She has the sweetest voice and just the cutest accent...

**To let myself free...**

In love
Love that is true
I have found you
And all that I wish for

**Stop!**

One of my favourite things I used to do on the ship was to

stand outside alone at night and stare up to the stars with the breeze which passed my face and threw my hair around wild while I would look again to see the elements of nature at her best as she reflected the rest of the sky in water.

## Where are you going?

The ship had amazed me although it was rather strange to familiarise with a living which required to keep on moving all of the time... really? No, the ship suited me perfectly with the lifestyle I was now to enjoy most. To stay in one place, I was not to enjoy because it soon enough became boring, unexciting, tedious, monotonous, repetitive, unnecessarily dramatic and, at times, dumb. Dumb in the sense of not having much new to learn: same people — same conversations — same places — and the same weather!

It was every three months, more or less, that I would move from one place to another, one job to another, one social circle to another. I did not do this because each place was bad either, many of them were to be pretty good actually. Some of them, not so much. The reason I did this is because I had wanted to keep on learning, keep on experiencing all the different ways life can be. I think life can be understood in an infinite amount of ways and no one way is the only way, so why not live as though there are many?

So, being on the ship was great for me with the travelling and everything. We were to port out of Florida and adventure around the islands of the Caribbean. Wow, can you possibly believe how much of the world I have seen now? I have not even the chance to mention most of it yet. I am so incredibly lucky: Key West, Puerto Rico, Antigua, St Lucia, Curacao, Aruba, Cayman Islands, Honduras, Guatemala and Mexico.

There is no place I do not want to go but this many countries and continents already?

## It was going good!

I loved how we were all to be from so many different backgrounds, from all across the world, and together we were working in the pursuit of happiness.

## So good!

All of the dancers on the ship were incredibly hot and unbelievably talented, yet I was lucky enough to be with the dancer I had thought most!

## Imagine.

Morning kissing
Midday dreaming
Night time wishing

## Will you?

And I am always thinking.

## Please realise!

Just how beautiful you are.

## Are you not always to get everything that you are to want?

The ship was to have it all and I was quite a fan of the elegance actually. Twice a week we were to have a black and white night, or something relatively similar, where everybody would dress up in their finest dining attire and spend the evening in one of the more luxurious restaurants before making it across to the theatre to end the evening being entertained.

As I was one of the photographers onboard, I was to circle around the ship on these occasions, taking a many great pictures for any guests who were willing to purchase a moment and a memory. However, the girl was to be one of the dancers in the evening entertainment shows and goodness knows if I was allowed to or not, but every time I would leave to go and watch her.

### She is an example of exactly that!

The way she could dance, the way she could move, there is nothing before which has caught my attention more, because the way she could dance, the way she could move, moved me like no other, I could not help but love her because the way she could dance, the way she could move expressed everything that life means to me, why I am to continue on and not give up.

### Right?

To see a light
I see a light
To see the truth
I see the truth

### She is the light.

This one day we had down in Puerto Rico... it was one of the best days of my life, although it was not real... because I had spent the entire day swept up in this kind of déjà vu where everything just seemed to be right, just seemed to be perfect... I was somehow to have this reassurance which flowed through me like the sound of a thousand angels in harmony, like a message from the gods who watch over me... It seemed as though it was all supposed to happen, it was all supposed to happen and that I am all right, that life will continue to be all right if I am just to let it be and I should not be afraid, not afraid of who I am, of where I am going and who I am going with... I am not alone. I have never been alone, even though I have thought myself to be. This voice, this voice was telling me every single thing that I had wanted to hear — that I was near to what I am to consider happiness... This one day we had down in Puerto Rico... it was no more than a dream and within the dream I was with a girl, the girl who I love... I always will.

**The angel.**

She had this something about her which seemed different to everyone else.

**Who knows?**

She was all of the time fascinating because she knew something I did not.

**How to.**

If there is anybody in life who knows how to change my life then it is her.

**Love.**

She made me laugh
She made me smile
She showed me heaven
She showed me love

**And the truth.**

I miss the way. Her way. She was to be. With me. And the little notes. She wrote. Stuck to my door. I saw. With a big smile. The best. She was the best.

You know. These messages. I should not say. She knew. What could I do? One answer. I had one answer. Of course. I had no doubt. None whatsoever.

Out of this world. This girl. This girl had me. No really. She had me completely. How unbelievable. Could it be true? I knew. She was the best.

**That is all I can say!**

It continued, we sailed for nine days across the Atlantic Ocean and got to see the Azores before travelling further onto, and reaching: Belgium, France, Spain, Portugal and Gibraltar. It was great fun although short-lived. However, we were to see many a great place, such as Cadiz and A Coruna. Lisbon was good and the Rock of Gibraltar was something, Bruges amazing but France, France, I still need to make peace with, to be honest. Yet, all of these places were nothing like what I was to see and experience in Norway and Iceland. Utterly breath-taking… that is all I can say!

**She knows how to love!**

She made my twenty-third birthday something special, that is for sure. Actually, it was probably the best birthday I was ever to have celebrated.

**And so do you!**

So, if there is anything in life which means more to me than this, I had made my decision and my decision was to, as

I always do, follow my heart.

## She really means everything to me.

It was not going to be much longer before her contract on the ship finished. At this time, I was only, not even, half way through my own contract and it had meant that she would soon to be going back to America whilst I was supposed to be going, thereafter, with the ship onto the Mediterranean, through the Suez Canal, around Asia, before ending the tour in Singapore.

I had really wanted to visit all of these places and to stay on the ship because I was actually good at my job — I could have, perhaps, progressed later to the position of manager — but I was also, and more importantly, to remember where I was exactly before my luck had changed from something which was killing me into something which has proven everything to me.

Honestly, why is it that change has to happen and so often? Anyway, I had to make a decision, should I stay or should I go? And it was my decision, it was totally my decision. She had not done anything other than say that... Apart from getting to know me in the first place... Not that it was her fault! But knowing... Could it have been possible to stay on the ship without her?

## The girl.

I had left the ship and with only three weeks to do it, and without any plans made beforehand, I had managed to organise a place to stay, a place to work and how I was going to try and make it back to America with her.

Unfortunately, it was only going to be for three months because of the visa requirements, but three months with her was worth so much more than a lifetime with anybody else I could have quite possibly imagined back then.

## My beautiful dancer.

You have no idea
Since we first met
You have meant everything to me
Your hair
Your eyes
Your smile
Your love
I cannot explain
The way you move
The way you make me feel
Out of this world
You take me there
Carry on
My beautiful dancer
Among the stars
I see you there
One day
I am going to be
The one that you want
In your arms
Hold me close
You have nothing to fear
Your life
Will be full of everything
All that you ever wish for
There will be a time
I will not let you down

Have faith
Be who you are
I believe in you
I always have
Teach me
Show me your secret
How do you do it?
Such grace
Everybody knows
To live life
The way you do
How amazing
I need to learn
Kiss me
Make love to me
Do all that you want
I will be there for you
My love
You have
Take it
Whenever you are ready
We can be together
I promise you everything

# Chapter Fourteen

**Her.**

Don't be afraid, he told me.

**Him.**

Love is all I live for.

**Her.**

Make the change happen. Don't wait for somebody else to change it for you. Find a way to do what it is you are to love. There is always a way to do it. Don't give up. Don't waste what you have. And don't tell yourself you can't. Don't hate what has been. Don't hate what the future will be. Just change.

**Him.**

It's too much. I can't. Not anymore. No. I am done. I am done now. Just done.

**Her.**

It may be difficult to recall your past but it is harder to forget it altogether.

**Him.**

There is no story unless it can be told.

**Her.**

You have one certain choice in this life and that is either to love it or not.

**Him.**

Rush not into anything except those things which you are to honestly love.

**Her.**

No matter how hard you will try
No matter how far you will go
No matter how much you will believe
Do you think it is your choice?

**Him.**

Have you ever stopped to consider and realise the importance of dreaming?

**Her.**

Wake up: everything you are to want is everything you are already to have.

**Him.**

It was the most difficult way to be
Wanting to give her everything
Knowing she did not need anything
And that it was me who was the one
Who could have done
More with everything I am now to see.

**Her.**

Happiness is not something you are to find, it is something

you are to have.

**Him.**

We are all living intelligent lives without being too intelligent about them.

**Her.**

If there is something
That you cannot believe in
It will not matter too much
To you, if it is real or if it is not –
For everything you are to experience
It will not be real, it will not
Exist; unless there is something

**Him.**

Have we only started to realise now just how truly valuable we really are?

**Her.**

In the blurriness, vision is only achieved by those who have gained focus.

**Him.**

If I was not to see her
It did not have to be long
Even if it was just a day
It felt as though I was lost

**Her.**

The best kind of education is self-education and for that you need others.

**Him.**

It is those gifts which you are giving without realisation that are the best.

**Her.**

If we were to remember
Everything which is to happen
Those things which will
Will never not
And it is important to ask
If we were to know those things
Why would they happen again?

**Him.**

We all have the ability to enable a rediscovery and remember who we are.

**Her.**

The hardest part is trying to forget who I am and who I am to be here with.

**Him.**

We were to have it all
This amazing house
This little dog
Near to London
The garden was huge

**Her.**

We were to have it all

One and other
Us two together
Our certain something
It was the dream

**Him.**

We were to have it all
For a while
Only two weeks
Just before America
I shall never forget

**Her.**

Everything is always moving… everything!

**Him.**

My insanity is only to save yours, my love.

**Her.**

It is not what is, it is the way of what is.

**Him.**

I had gone back with her
Back to her home, in America
Three more months we were together
How I wish it was forever

**Her.**

To pay with your love is a far greater expense than any value of money.

**Him.**

You are very much those who you will choose to surround yourself with.

**Her.**

There is something for me
And to find it I know where
But I cannot get there alone
I will need all of you to help

**Him.**

There is something for you
And to find it you know where
But you cannot get there alone
You will need all of me to help

**Her.**

God may seem to be cruel, but is he? Has he not given to us everything?

**Him.**

Throughout history in its entirety, has every human not searched for God?

**Her.**

It does not matter
How much the sun
Will shine for you
If you are to
Choose not to notice

**Him.**

Remember, there is as much universe above as there is below.

**Her.**

Remember, there can be no light if there was to be no darkness.

**Him.**

I have done wrong.
I could not help
Myself from doing so
And I will not
Be able to forgive
Myself from that I
Had done to her,
Her family and friends.
It was not me.
I can only apologise
For that I had
Needed to live out
But it is now
That I am to
Know what is true
And I am to
Promise it to you
I will never need
To do that again.

**Her.**

Blue and blue, the sea and you.

**Him.**

The sea and me, how can it be?

**Her.**

I now recall
Who I am
This place
This time and space
Just like heaven
Just like hell
It sure is
A good way to be
Why it is
So to know

**Him.**

Life is not what you are to do, it is what you are to do with real intent.

**Her.**

This incredible thing, life, gives us no greater pleasure than to be in unity.

**Him.**

I didn't want to go
I didn't want to leave
I didn't want to know
I didn't want to believe
Why would I want this?
I didn't want to fly

I didn't want to miss
I didn't want to say goodbye
I didn't want to give a last kiss

**Her.**

We could not know what home is if we were not to leave it to begin with.

**Him.**

Am I to believe in that we can call free will or, if we may call it so, God?

**Her.**

Together we have joined.

**Him.**

And together we shall part.

**Her.**

To express that which is in our mind.

**Him.**

And to express that which is in our heart.

**Her.**

There is a significant difference between being kind to another and trying to please another. It is very important to be kind and to be kind to yourself.

**Him.**

To speak the truth, the only thing which is really ugly in

this world is the way we can allow ourselves to treat ourselves, and sometimes it can be a lot, unkind.

**Her.**

I love you, I love you. I don't want to feel guilty, I just want to experience life as much as I possibly can. Is this wrong to do? No? I sincerely hope so.

**Him.**

The best, and most important, lesson I have learnt over the years is: the more you know, the less you know and all that you need to know is love.

**Her.**

When fear is to arise, think of love, for you will soon find yourself with the silliest smile, a somewhat embarrassing laugh and the company of friends.

**Him.**

The red, white and blue
And the sea between two
Separates me from home, you.

**Her.**

This life is quite like the game of hide and seek.

**Him.**

Everything, I would
I could, everything
Everything, I should
For her, everything

**Her.**

I can only be hopeful, there is no real certainty.

**Him.**

She is, the girl,
From St. Louis, Missouri
And I am to
I am to love
This girl so much

**Her.**

Life, I can promise you, has never let me down.

# Chapter Fifteen

**Love.**

It's the only thing I live for yet I am to know it'll be the very death of me.

**Yes?**

Have you ever considered the possibility of your dreams fading to nothing?

**Please.**

All I have been doing is trying to get back to America, that is what I want.

**For me.**

I had made it back to the United Kingdom and again I had no place to go. A few friends were to let me stay for a night or two, here and there, yet it was to become somewhat difficult because I had managed to take a job in the centre of London and the job was to be quite demanding, also rather time-consuming... meaning all of the travelling, here and there, was tough.

The plan was to try and make it through until the first pay check and then, hopefully, find a place, in which I could afford in central London, to rent for myself and, more importantly, a place I could try to call home. Well, as I have said, that was the plan. A nice plan though it was, unfortunately, no fortunately, it did not materialise because I had quit.

The job that is. You see, as much as I had wanted to live the 'normal' life it only took the first taste, the first idea of what it may be like, to scare me almost to death. To have my life planned out ahead of me; to be in a secure — a comfortable position financially; to know what I will be doing most days, other than a few weeks per year holiday, routinely; no thanks.

I am also lying quite a lot here. I was to start this new job only a week or so after leaving America and there was no way whatsoever that I could have possibly held down a job such as this with my mind pretty much still on the other side of the Atlantic Ocean. For a month, I had endured this predicament: I know that I have to move on but to move on I cannot.

**Don't leave.**

I didn't want to leave her. And I didn't want to leave America. I didn't want to be on my own. And I didn't have a place to call home. No. Yes, I did. I had her. But not any more though, once again. And this time I had no choice when to run. I had wanted to stay. For the first time, I had wanted to stay! And I couldn't tell her that I had wanted to say. I couldn't. She was everything to me. The other half of me. Without her, I am lost. Gone. Fallen. Beaten. No! Yes, I didn't want to leave. I had to leave. For her. For me. And for America. It wasn't to be. Not then. I wasn't to know home.

**Honestly?**

I don't like to think of it this way but is love nothing else than an excuse?

**You know.**

I had turned her against me. It was difficult. The situation made me crazy.

**Sometimes, this is the way it has to be.**

I had found myself in a position where I was ready to give everything up.

**You see.**

I had gone back to her, in America
For Christmas and New Year's Eve
I was to know, I could not let her go
For it was unbearable to try and leave

**Look at you.**

She had told me not to drink so much. She had wanted our last night together to be something special. She had told me not to drink so much...

But you know me. How stupid I can be, and you know me. How much I did not want to go, and you know me. I choose to escape when I lose out on life.

**Are you happy?**

I was such a fucking idiot, she absolutely fucking hated me. In the morning when I did not wake up to go and catch my fucking flight, she slapped me in the face and told me to fucking sort myself out. I had to fucking go. She drove me early at seven thirty to a fucking airport I cannot remember. It was the first of January and she kicked me out of the fucking car. I could not even fucking stand up properly when I was out of the car, she gave me this look I will never be able to fucking forget. It fucking killed me. She did not want to have anything more to fucking do with me. I could not even say goodbye to her and I do not even remember if we had a last kiss. I was such a fucking idiot, no really, she absolutely fucking hated me. That was it.

**Do you really think you are to know love?**
I have never experienced anything so painful;
my heart had been broken.
And it was made worse because I couldn't hate;
I was made to realise love.
The girl hadn't done anything to hurt me, intentionally;
only did I know.
She was to love me more than anybody else had;
when she had let me go.

**Speak truthfully.**
Contorted, twisted, tortured, stretched;
My body, my mind, my spirit, my love.

**Tell me.**
It is pretty damn hard to think that everything you believe in has gone.
Gone where?
That is the point... I do not know... But it is not... It is not here...
Then where?
It is pretty damn hard to think that everything you believe in has gone.

**Speak up!**
If you have not realised it already then there will be a time

soon, and what I am to talk about here is that life is just impossible to walk alone.

## You are not alone.

Only seventy-five years ago we would have been, or made to have been, against one another in a war which took madness to a whole other level.

It is madness to think that only seventy-five years on from what was to be a catastrophic, also necessary, disaster we, the world, have learnt from it...

Perhaps not all of us but at least most of us... Certainly my friend who I had met when out in South Africa. He is, seriously, up there with the best.

He is not South African — he is German. Well, he is originally from Germany; he has travelled, and lived, in various countries and continents.

A scientist, to be more precise, a biologist. My friend, well, my brother, is actually old enough to be my father yet he lives life younger than most.

He loves it, I mean he cannot get enough of it, which surprises me a lot. It surprises me because his life is so similar to mine, it is quite unbelievable.

Different though we are, and that is a great thing, he has taught me what it is to be alive. He has led me to realise that I am not alone. I never was...

## Come on!

I had to get out of the city and quick, I had needed those fields of freedom. My friend, sorry, my brother I shall refer to him from now on, had said I could go and stay at his place, on his sofa, for a few weeks in this village which was to be in the middle of nowhere and at the end of the trainline somewhere in the county of Wiltshire. Another county to add to a list of six…

My brother had moved to England about a year after South Africa, as he was dating a girl and had career prospects over here. And although he was living over here for the best part of three until this point, we would only occasionally meet up, perhaps two or three times per year, and most often for a late night out in whichever city was to be in-between the two of us.

Those nights were always pretty crazy, pretty funny, however, the point is that we had not really spent a huge amount of time to truly know one another, and it was easy for him to say, of course, with the permission of his girlfriend as they were living together, 'Yeah man, come and stay down here for a while until you can get yourself into a position to go forward…'

Within a couple of days, I had made my way down to this village. It was perfect. It was exactly what I had needed; it could not have been any more than what it was to be. Surrounded by fields upon fields and with a canal which flowed through its centre; this place was picturesque, peaceful and probably only another dream for me but, whether it was or not, I had to go.

**No.**

The thing is, all I had wanted was to forget. Forget the world and leave.

Go.

Elsewhere.

Somewhere.

Anywhere.

I did not care.

Fuck off — I did care.

Yeah?

No.

You were once somebody, now you are nobody. You are a waste of space. And you are a dumb cunt.

You want to?

Go.

Lose yourself with those drugs.

## I don't know anything, any more.

The colours, God

They amazed me

I hadn't seen anything like it before

It was like a dream

The blues, the different kinds of light

Everything was alive

Everything in unison

There was no pain

There was no effort

I could understand all I was looking over

It was like a dream

There I was talking again with my mother

Everything made sense

Everything was perfect

## Please, can you just leave me alone?

Like it is in every English village, there was a pub for the locals to gather. We had started going, most nights, to the local one here and it was friendly enough to keep on going back.

Well, it was most likely because they had beer that we had kept on going back to begin with, but soon enough we, my brother and I, got to know, it is always good to know, the landlord.

I would say a young man, to be a landlord, although he really could talk. And I liked the fact that he could talk because it was not so much about the things he happened to say, but rather the fact that he was opening himself up to anyone and everyone who was ever to enter the door looking for a little company and, of course, a drink. Though, never was it a drink.

### Please, just let me go.

To begin with, the drugs worked. The drugs were good, I had great times. They were to take me to these places that I had never been before, I think. Places that I had needed to go and go because I was never to realise how. The drugs were able to lift, if only slightly, the weight off my shoulders.

### Will you just fuck off!

A rat had crawled under my pillow and in front of my face it squeaked, it squeaked. It squeaked and stayed there, stayed there rubbing its face clean and staring at me. Staring at me with these little, beady, black-coloured eyes all bright,

I had freaked out, I had pushed it out, out of the bed but it had come back to me and this time with its family. There were four rats, two smaller ones which expressed their tiny faces as if to say that they had just been misled,

They did not want to be pushed out of bed. It was a fall too unbearable for them because they were only small, but what was I to do when they started crawling all over me, like I was a part of their family? I had turned away,

I had closed my eyes and repeated out loud that it was

only hallucinations in my head, the rats are not real, even though I could still feel their fur brushing against my skin, the rats are not real, the rats are not real, rats,

A spider started to crawl along the ceiling and directly above my head it stopped, it stopped and decided to descend down towards my face with its eight, hairy, spindly legs dangling around in anticipation to make contact,

As it got closer, the spider got bigger, but big as in the size of something like a tarantula, its body was huge and I could see all the details in its face. Its legs, one by one, started to touch upon me, and suddenly, I had punched it,

I had punched it so hard it disappeared, it disappeared but, then it seemed like it was the wrong thing to do because then all these other uglier spiders started to appear on the ceiling, each of them making their way over to me,

I had closed my eyes and repeated out loud, they were only hallucinations in my head, the spiders are not real, even though I could still feel their legs running, tickling my body, the spiders are not real, the spiders are not real,

Spiders kept on coming towards me, it felt as if I was trapped, as if there was nothing I could do to stop what was happening until this strange something, this spider I had punched so hard, had made its way through,

Through these different fragments of time and space, I could see it happen, I saw it happen. This spider went through this web-like net of what seemed to be an infinite, a perfect pattern I cannot describe,

Yet for every layer, for every layer the spider had broken into a roaring array of colours, would set out like wildfire to these lines in the pattern. Auburns, bronzes and golds lit up for me to see, the spider slowly fading away from reality.

**Be careful what you are to wish for.**

I had managed to get another photography job on a cruise ship and it was scheduled to head back over to America. However, when getting onboard I just could not handle it, being on a cruise ship without her was nothing but a prison for me, it was not even funny. I had gone completely insane. I had to leave the ship as soon as it was possible, that was to be in Norway.

We had got to Norway and I had to walk away. Walk away and then climb to the top of a mountain. All alone, I looked out to the spectacular view but the only thing on my mind was her, the girl, my beautiful dancer. We were once here together, we were once here together, and in love. I have never been happier in all of my life as then, back when, with her. She is everything.

**My dearest.**

Only when I am to think 'this is it', something, somebody will reappear once again to tell me another thing different and that is always the same. The same thing, every time. And in that moment, when I could have said 'enough is enough' and jumped, something, somebody had come into my life and told me it was not, that there is never enough of what this is to be.

**I know that you are to care.**

Eventually, I had called for help. I had called some of those who were very dear to me, who had looked after me in the past and it was so hard to ask knowing the state I was in, the state I had got myself into. I was not doing it to seek sympathy, I knew I needed help. So much so I had called a helpline and they had referred me, pretty much immediately, to visit a psychologist.

**I am not so sure.**

It was arranged. Finally, I was going to seek some professional help. It is something I should have done years ago but never did, not after that incident with the therapist when I was younger; I could not trust again…

**I don't trust anyone, any more.**

On the day of my appointment, I woke up early enough to do some drugs. An old friend had kindly offered to drive me to the hospital and, although I do have great respect for him, our friendship was extremely difficult. He liked to drink, a lot. As did I, but then I did drugs and he saw a difference.

Not long before he had arrived, my appointment was cancelled due to the doctor being sick and there not being enough other doctors. I do not know what he was thinking — if he was thinking I was lying. I do not know but the way he, my old friend, had acted, it seemed as though it was my fault!

**And I went back.**

Yes, it was not
An easy choice to
Make. It hurt to
Remember those days with
My family and with
My friends. It was
One place I could
Almost call home yet
Home is to be
No such thing, is

It? They didn't let
Me in. Not when
They had found out
That I was doing
Drugs. Yes, I was
Taking a lot of
Drugs but they did
Not understand nor did
They ask me why
I was doing something
Which is essentially self-harm
And I went back
There because I had
Needed them. I had
Needed help. Thank you.

## Because you need help!

Have you ever considered death to be the easiest way to get out of this mess?

## We still love you.

Only do I know so well that nothing good comes easy... Why am I still here?

## I was kicked out!

After the attempt of reaching out for help, it seemed as though I was to be in an even weaker position and far more desperate than I had been before. It was not only that I had no place to stay any more but I had also lost all desire to survive. It was at that moment I was ready to give up. No really. I was at the same train tracks as those the man said he would kill himself.

It would have been easy to do, to jump in front of one of the fast passing trains with nobody around to stop me. Oh, the memories. The memories of that place. Gone. The memories of my family. Gone. The memories which have brought me so much pain throughout these years: GONE. How nice that could have been? No? Why not? Why would I want to endure on with this?

## Can you not see?

I never thought I would do it. But I did. I had to. I had to feel something. I had to sin for something. I had taken the sharpest knife. Cut open my arm. One slice. Then it was twice. I could not care. I kept on going. There was no stopping. I liked these lines. I liked this pain. It felt nice. I wanted to dare. I was rolling my own dice. Life. Fuck it. I have tried and they have all lied.

## They all blame me!

It was the worst
It was so horrible
This dream I had
She had left me
She had no choice
She had to go
She was made to
Her parents had said
Just let him go
They were smart enough
They were to know
I was not right

I was only trouble
It was the worst
It was so horrible
What made it terrible
Was where it happened
She had left me
At the same house
My mother had cancer

**For crying out loud.**

It really is ridiculous, in many ways unbelievable, because when going back to this village in the middle of nowhere, in Wiltshire, all I had wanted was to escape away from everything. Escape away from all the things that had, even though I was to love them, fucked me up, each with their own purpose and reason. Of course, there was purpose and reason...

I hope. I only hope there was purpose and reason for everything because it is why I keep on going. Love may be how, but for what do I happen to love? Obviously, I am to need it and it is always there when I do. It always shows up strong. It always shows up stronger even when I want not to believe in it. In this village lived a girl and this girl was, in almost every way, perfect.

**Please listen to me.**

You know it is
This is how it is
This is how
It is all to begin

Those big-hearted people
Where are they to go?
Where are they?
Have we scared them away?

I had thought love
Love I had thought right
Love I had
That which is killing me

It is killing me
It is killing me because
Because I know
We need love to live

**This has to change.**

I knew the drugs would get the better of me eventually
and already, mentally… well, I never was stable really. Let's
say it was not sustainable. Even though the highs were worth
my neutral lows, I was to know that too many blows to the
head, to the brain will take me to the next level, will turn me
insane and that, in the end, will be the worst, the ultimate pain.

You see, those who are, who have been, insane I really do
have quite a lot of admiration for because they, I believe, for
the most part, were searching for something which, even if
they had finally found, was a lost cause. Not entirely but
mostly, especially during their lifetimes anyway because they
are never to be taken seriously, they are only ever
misunderstood, rejected.

And that, for me, is the hardest part to deal with, rejection,
being misunderstood, living a lonely life not because you want

to but because you have to. Because you are to know that life is so good, it is not something you are wanting to waste and you know that the best way to live is to be yourself but nobody, nobody around you can allow you to be you.

It really fucking sucks, believe me. Is it better to live a longer, more peaceful life as somebody else, or to live a shorter, more chaotic life as yourself? It is quite a good question to ask but if you are to answer with the latter, can you do it? My brother had gone back to Germany to visit the last of his family and he had asked me, nicely, if I was ready to move on.

For sure, he was not kicking me out but he was having some difficulties of his own with his girlfriend. There was not very much space at all in the house we were living in and as I was to be sleeping on the sofa downstairs, I was to be rather in the way. And dare I say, I was not waking up in the morning. The idea of waking up was completely and utterly unbearable.

## Together, we will change.

I have known for years that my experiences have caused my way of thinking to be somewhat, some would say, different. It is that I could even be labelled as 'mentally ill' to those who see society as fit. I have to say though, it is quite difficult to admit so I just keep on fighting, alone.

## Please, please help me.

The thing is, by taking those drugs I did get to leave. I did go. I had escaped. Yet, it was only ever momentary and the consequences were extraordinary. For every second of ecstasy I was to suffer an hour in anxiety, in deep piety. Apologising to God, trying my best with the devil, not wanting any trouble.

## What are you to want?

The landlord did not let rooms out at the pub however he was to make an exception. He said that he had wanted to help me, that he had the space and I was to need the space to collect my thoughts together and, with that, try and get better. My brother was to be just around the corner and there were a few spare shifts on the bar until I could find something permanent. The landlord was to become a very good friend.

## I had no choice.

Almost every night for almost six months I had to stay awake because I became too paranoid to sleep. It was unusual for me not to be able to sleep, because as I have said before, I really could sleep wherever I had wanted to. But there was this feeling which surrounded me and, dreadful it was, because the feeling created a sense of attack, a sense of aggression, to the extent that I had thought, at any moment given, something bad would happen and there would be nothing I could do about it.

However, just in case it did, I would continually prepare myself mentally, and this made everything so much harder to deal with as then I would spend most hours between twelve and six, hiding in my bathroom, listening to music and smoking as many cigarettes as it was possible, only to try and calm the fuck down! You know, there were times when I was to see things move, like flitter around in the darker areas of my bedroom, and I could never really work out what exactly any of it was.

## I want to talk with you, God.

God?

Yeah, you. I want to talk with you.

Me?

I think it is time that we have this.

I agree.

I am so high right now. I am sorry.

Sorry?

I know I should not be doing this.

Really?

No, I do not know what I am doing.

It is quite funny.

Why on earth would you say that?

You run around pretending.

I run around because I do not belong.

Tell me, what do you not belong to exactly?

There is no place or no one who wants me.

No place? No one? You really are lost!

I am, God! I am going out of my mind!

This is it, this is precisely it.

Do you not think I am going out of my mind?

Oh no, you are.

You say that as if you do not care whatsoever.

That is not true.

So, why do you not do anything to help me then?

I do. The question is, do you?

## Because.

I thought it was a good idea to take a sobriety. For five months I did not drink; I did not smoke; I did not take any drugs; I ran six kilometres every other day without fail and I had a great diet but it all left me so lonely, it had left me to spend most of my time alone because everybody else was socialising together and drinking, smoking, taking drugs and everything…

**You know.**

This girl and I, we got along like a house on fire. It was so much fun…

**I love…**

I think I can admit to this, this girl I had not known long saved my life.

**The girl.**

This girl, I wanted to love this girl but there was something stopping me.

# Epilogue

**You know I love this life.**

Coming into life is now something I do keep possession of in my memory. I do ask myself if it is necessary to know such an experience and I know it is completely. However, I do know, and keep memory of, life coming into me.

**You know all the reasons why.**

I have said many things
Things which expose myself
Things which bring vulnerability
To who I am and my personality
Though, there are certain things
Which I cannot tell you
And there are very good reasons why

**I cannot keep on doing this.**

I have to make the change happen, I cannot keep on going out of my mind.

**All on my own, without you.**

He was to know his every action if only he did not doubt himself so much.

**In all that I can do.**

I have always worked wherever I have been and that is

how I can afford it. It is also true that I have never claimed a single benefit other than a given bursary at university and that is something I am proud of, because for me, nobody can judge against how I have used my money, it is not theirs. And yes, I have been extremely fortunate to have known so many giving people.

## It is absolutely nothing, without love.

I am not lost. I am just another who knows love and what life is without it.

## We all need one another.

Nothing can be without its other, its opposite living only to make it better.

## We have to stand up, together.

My brother and I have really got to know one another over this past year. It is he who has kindly helped me and all so subliminally realise reality.

## We are all in this, together.

I am starting to learn my lesson, because there is nowhere I can go to escape.

I have to face up to everything which has held me back. It is the only way.

## We will learn to forgive ourselves.

Somehow, I had thought it was a good idea to go on another cruise ship and this time as a host. Seriously? And I had got the job with one of the best cruise lines in the world... Why would I choose to do this to myself? Really? I had found myself touring all the islands of the Pacific Ocean as far out as Fiji and porting down in Sydney, where I was to have a friend.

An old friend I had met way back when in South Africa. She was a great girl, a great character who had helped me out a lot over the past few years. Her advice was always pretty damn good, even though, most often, I did not want to hear it... because so. The sad thing about our friendship though, I had jeopardised it a year earlier when she came to visit back in England.

It appears to be a talent of mine, doesn't it? To ruin all the good things which happen to me. It is like I am to do it on purpose, like I am to act as if I do not want all the good things to be in my life. And why? Tell me why would I want to be like that? Why? Do you think it is what I want? Interesting, isn't it? I know what I am doing but I can't help from doing it.

**We will learn to open up.**

Why have I not mentioned that when I was much younger, I was very lucky to visit the countries of Cyprus, Greece, Germany and Andorra?

**We will learn to move on.**

I've had opportunities to go back to America. I've managed to get other jobs which could have taken me there but there has always been one problem.

**We will start to behave better.**

It was horrible. It was painful. My sister and her husband turned on me, turned against me, hated me, told me they did not want to see me again.

**Our love, it really does matter.**

It turns out that my father had tried to manipulate them to believe I was the one in the wrong, that it was my fault: It is me, I am the one to blame!

**I love everybody in my life.**

I would not be anywhere without the help from the friends that I have.

All of the friends that I've had.

Those who are no longer to know me, that have left me.

And those whom I have left.

I am sorry that our paths had chosen to go in so very different directions.

I would not be anywhere without the help from the friends that I have.

All of the friends that I have.

Those who are still to know me, who are able to see me once in a while.

Are you to know that it is our friendship which carries me on through?

I am to know what we are to have will not last forever but I do thank you.

I would not be anywhere without the help from the friends that I have.

All of the friends that I am to have.

Those who are not yet to know of me and I am neither to know of them.

A time will come, believe in me, when we are to find one and other.

I am to say, however, all of my friends mean the same and everything to me.

### Now I need to love myself.

In so many ways I had tried to let go but no. No matter what I did, no matter what I had done, never was I to have won and the past would always beat me, one way or another, and there was nothing I could do to cover, to cover up my ongoing pain and suffering and hate and anger, no, it is only ever to get worse, it is like I am waiting, I am waiting to burst.

### Are you able to help me?

It would be interesting to receive professional help for my way of thinking. I have not even had a prescription to combat the battle of my 'mental illness' and it is not because a doctor will not offer it, it is in fact, the exact opposite. From my experience, it seems as though mental health is not much of anything, if nothing which cannot be dealt with by a number of tablets, and that, I believe, is wrong, so unbelievably wrong to go about something so serious.

### I am trying to help you.

To be homeless is not to be without a house, it is to be without yourself.

To be without a house is far and much different, that is to be houseless.

### And God is, he is too.

I am a long way from home and I miss the girl something crazy. What am I supposed to do now? Write a story — Seriously?

**Thank you, God — I love you.**

There are many things which happen to me
And I am almost certain that they have been done
On purpose because when these things are to happen
There is nothing I can do but smile and thank them
Who make my life something which I love so much

**So much so I only know.**

Those people may not be those people but they are who I
want them to be.

**You have given to us everything.**

Do we need to be fabricating beauty from the suffering of
the innocent?

**How can we love you enough?**

If you do not believe in equality, in fairness, then you are
a human racist.

**To be kind to our neighbour?**

Slavery of the mind is a slavery only by choice. What do
you really think?

**Shall we overcome hardship with humour?**

Like the weird and the wonderful… they will be the ones
you'll remember!

**I'm trying to be a writer!**

I call myself a writer
I do not know how to write

I call myself a lover
I do not know how to love
I can call myself lonely
No more do I let anybody in
I call myself a dreamer
The dream is still yet to begin

**Oh, how much I love her!**

Only when the work has been done then will it be time for us to go home.

**And how much I love you.**

Why? Why did I do this? This pain. This blame. Why? Why did I do this? To let you all know. To let everything go. Why? Why did I do this? To speak out loud. To an unknown crowd. Why? Why did I do this? It is not easy. Most of it kills me. Why? Why did I do this? I have a choice. To keep quiet my voice. Why? Why did I do this? We all know. But will it help though?

**God, I can say this, right?**

If there is to be an answer to everything then we are already to know of it.

**How else will you be able to return back home?**

Love. That is what I live for yet it will be the very death of me, I know it. And I say I am to know love, like I am to know myself, yet I have no idea what love is or who I am. All I do know is that love and I are inseparable.